I WANT
YOU TO
KNOW
WE'RE
STILL
HERE

Esther Safran Foer

I WANT YOU TO KNOW WE'RE STILL HERE

My family, the Holocaust
and my search for truth

ONE PLACE. MANY STORIES

HQ
An imprint of HarperCollins*Publishers* Ltd
1 London Bridge Street
London SE1 9GF

1

First published in Great Britain by
HQ, an imprint of HarperCollins*Publishers* Ltd 2020.
Published in the United States by Tim Duggan Books, an imprint of
Random House, a division of Penguin Random House LLC, New York.

A catalogue record for this book is
available from the British Library.

ISBN HB: 978-0-00-829762-6
ISBN TPB: 978-0-00-829765-7

Printed and bound by CPI Group (UK) Ltd, Croydon CR0 4YY

MIX
Paper from
responsible sources
FSC www.fsc.org **FSC C007454**

For my parents, and those who came before them.
For my grandchildren, and those who will come after them.

I WANT
YOU TO
KNOW
WE'RE
STILL
HERE

1

My birth certificate says that I was born on September 8, 1946, in Ziegenhain, Germany. It's the wrong date, wrong city, wrong country. It would take me years to understand why my father created this fabrication. Why, each year, my mother came into my room on March 17 and gave me a kiss and whispered, "Happy birthday."

Piecing together the fragments of my family story has been a lifelong pursuit. I am the offspring of Holocaust survivors, which, by definition, means there is a tragic and complicated history. My childhood was filled with silences that were punctuated by occasional shocking disclosures. I understood there was a lot that I didn't know, besides the secret of my invented birthday. My parents were reluctant to speak of the past, and I learned to maneuver around difficult subjects.

When I was in my early forties, preparing to give a talk at a local synagogue, I decided that this might be a good opportunity to fill in a few gaps of our family story. I sat down with my mother in the pink kitchen of her 1950s-suburban tract house, on a street where most of the other homes were occupied by families of Holocaust survivors. Sitting at her faux-marble laminate kitchen table, I could see the carefully cut coupons sorted into neat piles by the refrigerator, ready for the next shopping trip. In the cabinet below, there was enough flour and cereal, all of it purchased on sale, to withstand a major catastrophe.

I started with a few questions about my father and his experience during the war. He had been an enigma, a mercurial figure that all conversation danced around, even in my own head. My mother took a sip of the instant coffee that she loved and casually mentioned that my father had been in a ghetto with his wife and daughter. He'd been on a work detail when they were both murdered by the Nazis. Absolutely stunned, I blurted out, "He had a wife and daughter? Why haven't you ever told me this before? How can you be telling me now for the first time?"

I had grown up surrounded by ghosts—haunted by relatives who were rarely talked about and by the stories that no one would share. Now there was a new ghost that I hadn't even known about—my own sister. I pressed my mother for more, but she made it clear that the conversation was over. *Genug shoyn.* Enough already. I'm not sure how much she even knew about his family—I suspected that she and my father didn't speak much of the past, even to each other. Life was all about moving forward.

I walked out of my mother's house in a daze.

I didn't know it then, but this was the beginning of a search that would define the next phase of my life.

Determined to learn more, I scoured online Holocaust databases to see if I could find a birth or death record for my sister, to no avail. I hired researchers in Ukraine. I even hired an FBI agent to analyze photographs. My searches came up empty.

I talked to everyone I could think of to see what they knew, and I got the same response: "There were so many people killed, so many babies, how can we remember all of the names?"

I didn't want all of the names. I wanted the name of my sister.

Of the person closest to me killed in the Holocaust, my half sibling, I had not one detail, not a name, not a picture—not one piece of a memory. Here was a child, one among at least six million Jews, one of almost 1.5 million children who were murdered during the Holocaust, and there was no way to remember that this child had even lived.

How do you remember someone who has left no trace?

The search took me to places that allowed me to more deeply understand the Holocaust and how it continued to reverberate long past the liberation and into future generations. It was ultimately a search that took me to places inside myself that scared me.

It has been said that Jews are an ahistorical people, concerned more with memory than history. A curious fact: There is no word in the Hebrew language that precisely connotes history. *Zikaron* and *zakhor*, used in its stead, translate to "memory." The word for "history" in modern Hebrew is lifted from the English word, which was originally lifted from the Greek *historia*. History is public. Memory is personal. It is about stories and select experiences. History is the end of something. Memory is the beginning of something.

"Jews have six senses. Touch, taste, sight, smell, hearing . . . memory." This is the way my son Jonathan summed it up in his 2002 novel, *Everything Is Illuminated*. "The Jew is pricked by a pin and remembers other pins. . . . When a Jew encounters a pin, he asks: What does it remember like?"

Parsing this intersection of history and memory may seem an abstraction, a mere matter of linguistics, but for me it is quite real. I have spent much of my life trying to excavate the memories that elude me.

On the mantel in my living room is a curated still life of glass jars. A casual visitor to my home might think I have created a shrine to dirt and debris, and they wouldn't be entirely wrong. Inside each carefully labeled jar is a sliver of memory: a piece of earth from my mother's shtetl in Kolki, Ukraine; sandstone from the massive Uluru rock in Central Australia; remnants of the Berlin Wall; rubble from the Warsaw Ghetto. Once, on a trip to Sardis, Turkey, I noticed that a piece of the marble mosaic floor of an ancient synagogue had come loose, and I discreetly slipped a fragment of tile into my bag when my husband had turned the other way. Despite his frequent admonitions to please not abscond, let alone cross international borders, with my purloined ruins, my husband, Bert, knows that getting me to abide is hopeless. I'm an aggressive collector, a woman with a mission, who walks around stuffing pieces of personal history into Ziploc bags.

Memory is everywhere in my house. The twenty-one jars in my living room are part of a larger collection that spills into my kitchen, where along the window ledge are nearly forty more.

This obsession runs in my family. Who knows, it might even be genetic. As improbable as it sounds, the youngest of my three sons, Joshua, was the 2006 U.S.A. Memory Championship winner. It's a subject about which he wrote a book: *Moonwalking with Einstein: The Art and Science of Remembering Everything.* Frank, my oldest, a writer and historian, recently spoke on a panel in Kiev, Ukraine, our ancestral homeland, titled: "Can memory save us from history? Can history save us from memory?" Jonathan, my middle child, managed to elicit the words "holy shit" from fire inspectors who paid a routine visit to his dorm room at Princeton in the late 1990s, where they saw, along with the usual collegiate fire hazards of tangled electrical cords and DIY lighting, a collection of Ziploc bags carefully tacked to his wall in rows—his own receptacles of memory.

Even when entombed inside a jar, memory is both tangible and shape-shifting. Memories aren't static; they change with time, sometimes to a point where they bear only a passing resemblance to what actually happened.

Even so, I feel a great responsibility to keep the past alive.

"How will I know who these people are?" my oldest grandchild, Sadie, asked me one day, while we were sitting in my home office, which overflows with photographs, documents, and maps, some neatly organized in labeled boxes and others in piles around the room.

Sadie's question haunts me. I haven't bothered to identify the people in these photographs, because I know who they are. My mother, interestingly, took the time to label and categorize all of her pictures—not just the old ones, but even those of her children and grandchildren and great-grandchildren.

Sadie's query made me want to cast aside all other obligations and tend to my vast messy archive. In those crammed boxes, most of what is known of my family's past resides. The photos are all that remain of long-dead relatives with no direct descendants to tell their stories or even to remember their names. They are not just photos of those killed in the Holocaust but even of family in America, such as the one of my young cousin Mark, whose grandparents and parents took my parents and me in when we arrived in Washington, D.C., in 1949, after almost three years in a displaced-persons camp in Germany. Mark, an only child and an only grandchild, died shortly after this photograph was taken, after a routine tonsillectomy, at the age of four—just a few months before we came to the United States. We left behind the deprivations of the DP camp and the horrors of war only to slip into the wake of this other quiet tragedy. Now that his parents are gone, too, it is up to me to keep the memory of this wisp of a boy alive.

To know me, you would think I am a happy woman with an easy smile—which I am. But at the same time, my joy is tempered by the shadows of the past. In the darker corners of my mind live the ghosts who visit me from the shtetls in Ukraine where my family once lived, and where most of them died. Some of the details that make these visions so vivid are imagined, because I grew up in a family where memories were too terrible to commit to words.

My parents, Ethel Bronstein and Louis Safran, were the only members of their large extended families to survive the Holocaust. My mother spent the war on the run. I don't know how my father survived, although we know he was hidden by a family for at least some part of it. Their parents, siblings, nieces and nephews, aunts and uncles, and cousins were all murdered. I can't bring myself to use the common euphemism "perished."

Children can bring down walls and open doors for their parents. Jonathan's first novel, based on a journey to Europe before his final year of college, did just that. He was in search of a topic for his senior thesis, and I urged him to visit the shtetl Trochenbrod, in Ukraine, where I thought my father had come from. Before he left for Europe that summer of 1998, I gave him forty copies of a tattered black-and-white picture of four people—my father, an older man, and two women—the people who my mother thought had hidden him in their house for some part of the war. The hope was that Jonathan might find the family that gave my father shelter.

A black-and-white photo of my father, Louis Safran (top, left)
and the family that hid him during the war.

Jonathan found nothing. Lacking facts, he spent the rest of the summer writing a work of fiction based very loosely upon the few details we knew of our family history. The novel opened doors that filled in many of the most important memory holes in my life, as fiction mysteriously generated facts.

In Jonathan's novel, the self-declared hero, whose name is also Jonathan Safran Foer, is in pursuit of a character named Augustine, who is thought to have hidden the fictional Jonathan's grandfather. It is fiction layered on possible fact layered with more fiction. It's a dazzling, playful Rubik's Cube of a book that spins on its head our family history and leaves even me a tad confused. It's fiction, yes, but here Jonathan, unwittingly, had touched a nerve. My family's deeply buried memories, their tendency toward silence, would have its own tragic repercussions. Jonathan writes of a suicide that echoes one in our own family—something he was unaware of at the time that he wrote the book.

The release of the book, and the film that followed, sparked new interest in the shtetls our family came from and opened the door for new information from a variety of sources. My own obsession grew accordingly. I began working genealogy websites, picking up new clues during travel in Brazil and Israel.

There was only so much I could do from afar. Like the character in Jonathan's novel, I armed myself with maps and photographs and eventually boarded a Lufthansa flight to Ukraine in 2009. I brought with me, of course, a supply of Ziploc bags.

I set out to find the family that had hidden my father during the war and to see what I could learn about the sibling I had never known. I set out to find a shtetl that, by all accounts, was no more. I set out to learn about my father. I set out to know about my sister. I set out to let my ancestors know that I haven't forgotten them. That we are still here.

2

One morning in early July 1941, as Nazi parachutes rained down from the sky, as people froze and watched, or raced home to barricade themselves inside, or collected their families and prepared to hide, my mother decided to flee.

But first she ran back along the dirt road to her house to grab a pair of scissors, a few items of clothing, and her winter coat.

In my imagination, it was a beautiful, temperate summer day, but she nevertheless thought to take her winter coat, along with the scissors and a change of clothes. Her own mother stood by and watched in silence. They parted without saying goodbye.

My mother's younger sister, seventeen-year-old Pesha, ran after her, chasing her down the dirt road that led from their small wooden house to the main street of Kolki.

"You are so lucky to be leaving," Pesha said, as she took off her shoes and gave them to my mother so she would have an extra pair. Pesha then turned and walked home barefoot along the same dirt road.

My mother almost immediately lost one of the shoes.

This was one of the foundational stories I grew up with—Pesha and the shoes. My mother came back to this again and again. As with the stories about my father, she would every now and then let slip some astounding detail and then refuse to elaborate. *Genug.* Enough. It was too painful to recount, but in this case, I suspect her reluctance was infused with the guilt of leaving Pesha behind, of not saying goodbye to her mother. They were two strong-willed women, and there had been plenty of recent tension.

My mother Ethel with her younger sister Pesha, their grandmother Rose, and my mother's cousin Freika.

I wanted to know Pesha, to hear her, to see her, to know what she was like, but my mother wasn't willing to tell me more, other than repeating over and over again the story of the shoes. I have a photo of Pesha from when she was maybe five or six, standing between my mother and their maternal grandmother Rose. She is a cute, impish child, with short brown hair, wearing a shirt with a long bow, more a tie than a bow. She is holding her grandmother's hand. On the other side of their grandmother is my mother's cousin Freika. The photograph looks somewhat formal—or what passed for formal in those days—with a makeshift curtain in the backdrop, and it's the only photograph of Pesha that survives. The photo, with an inscription from my mother on the back, was sent to my mother's Aunt Chia in the United States. The few photographs I have were sent to American and Brazilian relatives. I am grateful because it is the only thing that enables me to see Pesha as something other than a ghost.

If you asked my mother how she survived the war, she would say it was luck and intuition. She was always on the lookout for four-leaf clovers. She visited fortune-tellers. Late in her life, she kept a pencil and paper with her to play inscrutable games of chance. Tiny scratchings, numbers that she jotted down and then crossed out, appeared at random on scraps of paper or even in the middle of greeting cards she received. A small table in her bedroom was full of elephants brought to her as gifts, their trunks tilted upward, a sign of good luck. She was full of old-world superstition: If you bragged about your good fortune around my mother, she would tell you that the evil eye, or *gatoyik* in Yiddish, would see you and bring on troubles.

So perhaps luck and intuition helped save her, but I know that it was more than that.

For most of her life, my mother didn't call herself a Holocaust survivor. In her mind, the term was reserved for those sent to concentration camps. My family was part of the Holocaust that people didn't know about or understand at the time. Of the six million Jews killed during the Holocaust, somewhere between one and a half and two million were rounded up from their homes in Eastern Europe and taken to open pits, where they were shot by *Einsatzgruppen*—German mobile killing squads—sometimes with the help of local collaborators. This is often referred to as the "Holocaust by Bullets."

From shtetl to shtetl, there were small variations in how the murders occurred. Sometimes Jews were first herded into ghettos and into forced labor. Some were led into synagogues that were then set on fire. Some were beaten to death, or raped, or forced to walk into open pits, or transported to their grave sites in trucks. Sometimes the graves were already dug; other times the Jews were required to wield the shovels themselves. The narratives differ in detail, but all end on the same unspeakable note.

So, yes, something bad was indeed coming, and my then-twenty-one-year-old mother was not relying entirely on her gut on the day that the Nazis invaded her shtetl. In addition to the parachutes, there were trucks rolling into the village, with soldiers in uniform. You might think others, even if they lacked my mother's intuition, would look at these signs and flee, as well. There was some warning—the incursion onto the Soviet territory had begun two weeks earlier, on June 22, at 4:00 A.M. on the dot. And yet, as we know from the tales of survivors, from our knowledge of history, from our understanding of human behavior, it was not easy to abandon a home, to spontaneously pack up and leave behind all that you had ever known. And even more difficult to imagine the fate that awaited if you did not.

My mother had another reason for knowing that it was

best for her to leave. As a teenager, she had been involved with a local Communist group, and she suspected this affiliation would not serve her well when the Germans arrived. She had once even been arrested, dragged out of her house in the middle of the night, taken to the police station in a horse and buggy, and thrown into jail. Her widowed mother had to send her son-in-law and a lawyer to get her out. When my mother finally came home, her mother wouldn't talk to her. That was her punishment and presumably part of what contributed to their steely farewell.

My mother would tell her grandchildren that she wasn't really a Communist, that she just believed in "equal rights." Nevertheless, we know that she went to meetings. Who knows—some of that might have even been self-protection, because whether it was the Russians or the Germans or the Ukrainians who were worse to the Jews had a fluid answer, dependent on the moment in time. And for a while at least, during the Russian occupation of Kolki from 1939 to 1941, she was rewarded by the Russians, first with a job in an office and then as a manager in one of the larger regional stores.

It's also possible that my mother's political leanings had to do with her resentment of her paternal grandfather. Shtetl life is rendered idyllic by Marc Chagall and turned into fable by Isaac Bashevis Singer, but one thing I have learned from piecing together my family narrative is that the place was just as full of drama—family tensions and divorce and unwanted pregnancies—as any modern-day soap opera.

Nissan Tzvi Bronstein, my mother's paternal grandfather, was one of the richest men in town. In addition to owning the flour mill that stood behind his large multigenerational house, he was an exporter of dried mushrooms and bristles for brushes. He was so wealthy that he even had a piano, which was quite a luxury at the time. He built up an international business, and about every six months he traveled to the United States for work and to visit his two children, Necha and Max, who had settled in St. Louis.

My mother and her sisters, Pesha and Lifsha, had been living in Nissan's house with their parents, Srulach and Esther, while their own house was being built. Then Srulach contracted tuberculosis. He hoped to travel to a sanatorium in Italy for a cure, but a visa was denied, so he and Esther headed west to a sanatorium somewhere near Warsaw, which is where he died.

When Esther returned from burying her husband, she and her father-in-law had a dispute; apparently, it had to do with the inheritance for her and her children now that her husband, Nissan's son, had died. The argument turned sufficiently bitter that my grandmother and her two daughters moved out and into their unfinished house. Lifsha, Srulach's daughter from his first marriage (his first wife had also died of tuberculosis), was sent off by her grandfather to live in another town with one of her aunts.

This resulted in such bad feelings that for the rest of her days in Kolki, my mother would cross the road when she walked down the main street so that she would not have to walk in front of Nissan's house. She tended to see the world in black and white and did not forgive easily.

Even when it was still difficult to get my mother to talk about the war, she would open up about Kolki, and detail by detail I was eventually able to construct a version of the shtetl in my mind. I could envision the houses, the animals, the stoves, my grandmother, and my aunts. I knew where everyone lived. I could see my mother in a fashionable dress that might have been sent to her by one of her American cousins, walking down to the river for a *shpatzir,* a stroll, with friends. Or she might have come down to the sandy banks, near the canoes, to wash the dishes before Passover.

Other stories began to emerge, often toggling between harrowing war stories and the minutiae of everyday life. The horrors become familiar with time, but the banal details can take on an almost magical quality, which might account for the instinct of artists to make the shtetl into a fairy tale.

It was a wonderful little town with nice people. Plain people. Hardworking.

We had a library. We had a doctor. We had a dentist.

The houses were made of brick.

And of wood.

They were nice houses.

Next door to us lived two brothers.

They were butchers.

We had horses.

And wagons.

We had nice clothes and beautiful shoes.

On the Sabbath, there was chicken, beef sometimes, turkey maybe twice a year for the big holidays.

Schmaltz was a big thing. Here, you don't want the fat, you throw it away. There, when you go to the butcher—I remember this—they used to beg the butcher should give them a little bit of fat . . .

And Trochenbrod, where I went once in a while, in the summer, because there was everything: fresh milk, fresh sour cream, like yogurt. Smetana. From the smetana you made butter . . . Very tasty . . . everything was fresh there, fruits . . .

We continued to press my mother for details, sometimes conducting formal interviews. Frank decided to write about his grandmother for his high school senior project, and over the course of six weeks in 1992 he spent several days each week with her, a tape recorder running as he took her shopping, with all of those coupons in hand, in search of that week's bargains. She has also been interviewed by volunteers from the U.S. Holocaust Memorial Museum, by writers and filmmakers, by other family members, and by an anthropologist cousin, who was interested in details on Kolki. I have hours and hours of taped interviews done during different stages in her life.

There were recurring motifs: the winter coat, the sister who ran after her, the pair of shoes. Beautiful Lifsha, my mother's twenty-five-year-old half sister, and Lifsha's two daughters, and her husband, David Shuster, who had been conscripted into the Polish army to fight the Nazis.

My mother remembered going with Lifsha and the rest of the family to see David off. "We all cried and cried," my mother said, "because we thought we might never see him again."

David survived; Lifsha and their daughters did not. Lifsha was killed in such a terrible way that my mother hesitated to speak of it, until she did, cryptically, referring to a million rapes. It's not entirely clear to me when Lifsha died, but from what I have been able to piece together, she was one of the first killed in the initial days of the invasion, as was my mother's maternal grandfather, Yosef Weinberg. He had been in one of the four synagogues in the village for morning prayers when the Nazis came. The doors were bolted and the synagogue set on fire.

Pesha and her mother, Esther, and her paternal grandmother Chava, along with Lifsha's daughters, ages two and five, were taken to a ghetto set up for Jews, where they survived for about a year. Pesha managed to sneak out of the ghetto to see whether she could trade some silver spoons for food for the family and was shot on sight. Not long after, Chava and Esther, each holding one of Lifsha's children in their arms, were shot over an open pit.

And then, amid the horror of these awful stories, my mother took a poignant detour:

Before the war, there had been a man. A dentist. He asked her to go for a ride in his canoe, but she did not go, even though she liked him. He came to visit her, but nothing happened—she seemed both intrigued and a little frightened by his attention. He was about ten years older—or maybe five or maybe twenty years older. The age gap seemed to vary with each rendering of the story, and once she opened up about it, I heard it many times. I might ask my mother a question about the river and it would lead her back to the dentist, the man who asked her to go with him for a ride in the canoe.

And here—in this man with his boat—it is possible to see the genesis of just about every sweeping wartime love story. Apparently, there was another, more serious boyfriend, who at some point later, after the war, after he enlisted to take revenge on the Nazis, after he was badly wounded, somehow managed to find Ethel's address, to write, or have someone else write, a postcard with the message: "Don't wait for me. Go and get married." And she did. She married and she buried her husband and then she married again, and somehow, after my mother had been maybe fifteen or twenty years in the States, this man's sister, remarkably, found Ethel and told her what had happened to him. "For two, three days I couldn't eat," my mother said.

What *had* happened to him? I don't know. It's one of many questions, another fragment of another story, that I'll never have an answer to.

Even with just these sketchy details, I can still imagine the scene, my mother overcome with emotion, now remarried, living in suburban America, running a grocery store. She has children and stepchildren; she has a complicated and in many ways difficult life. And now this unexpected news from the past, information about a long-lost love. I can see the telephone receiver pressed to her ear, her fingers nervously playing with the long looping cord.

She communicates with the sister for a while, clandestinely. But then, whatever it is that is going on, she decides to let it go.

"This is what happened," she says simply, years later. "You know, what a terrible war."

———

I would later learn this was only one of my mother's postwar suitors. David Shuster, who had been married to Lifsha, asked my mother to marry him after the war. This is an old Jewish shtetl tradition—a widower marries the unmarried younger sister. But my mother refused him; she told me she couldn't marry her sister's husband. David seemed to understand and was respectful of her answer—he even gave her money for a new coat.

They saw each other years later in Israel. By that time, David had remarried and he now had another daughter and a stepson. He told my mother that he always kept a hidden picture of Lifsha with him.

Kolki. It was a wonderful town, with nice, plain, hard-working people, my mother said.

In the prewar years, there were few cars. If one came through, everyone ran after it, because it was such a wonder.

There was no indoor plumbing and no electricity, except in two or three homes, including my great-grandfather's—the one with the piano.

The ovens provided heat.

Water came from the nearby Styr River or from wells. If you could afford it, water was delivered by a man who carried it in buckets on his shoulders.

Laundry was washed by boiling some of this water on the stove.

Wednesday was market day, when most of the shopping took place. My mother described it as a kind of bazaar or flea market, where you could see everything from horses and cows to blueberries and butter. There were little stores, usually attached to people's houses—tailors, shoemakers, bakers, carpenters—and a doctor and, of course, the dentist.

There were a number of different synagogues in Kolki—at least four small synagogues that my mother could remember, some organized by profession. For example, there was the schneider's shul (the tailor's synagogue) and one for the more prosperous merchants, like my mother's rich grandfather, and there were synagogues based on the rabbi's orientation. My mother, when asked, couldn't remember ever actually going into one of the synagogues, although she recalled playing outside during the Jewish High Holidays.

My parents were born in the same region—in what is now western Ukraine and was then eastern Poland—but not the same town. Trochenbrod and Kolki were only about thirteen miles apart, and there were lots of family overlaps and visits between the towns.

There really is such a thing as Jewish geography. If you are a member of the tribe, you learn not to express surprise when you realize that your next-door neighbor is related to your best childhood friend or that his daughter has just married your cousin. Or that the boy in your son's fourth-grade class is in fact a distant cousin.

"This town is a shtetl," you might say. Except it's more than just one town. It's the world.

My mother had an anecdote she liked to tell about a visitor from the United States who was walking down the street in Kolki when a woman stuck her head out the window and yelled to him: "Do you know my Benjamin? He lives in New York." As if America were such a small place that everyone knew everyone the way they did in Kolki. No punch line survives, but the answer could very well have been yes.

Like me, my mother had a confusing birth date. She knew that she was born in 1920 in Kolki on Lag B'Omer, a minor Jewish holiday that is considered a "happy day" in the middle of a period of sadness between Passover and Shavuot, a day for parties and bonfires. In the shtetl, dates were easy to mark if they coincided with a Jewish holiday. In 1920, Lag B'Omer fell on May 6. All of my mother's official documents from the displaced-persons camps and her U.S. citizenship papers, however, show a birth date of June 15, 1920. When I pressed her on why the mix-up of dates for her and for me, she said that my father did it—that he scrambled all of the dates. In retrospect, since he clearly changed my birth date intentionally, my guess is he decided to mix up the others, as well.

Stories handed down from one generation to another change our behavior, but whether that leads to a desire to learn more or to silence the past, who can say. This question is central to a body of thought called *postmemory*, a term first introduced by writer and Columbia professor Marianne Hirsch. The idea is that traumatic memories live on from one generation to the next, even if the later generation was not there to experience these events directly. She suggests that the stories one grows up with are transmitted so affectively that they seem to constitute memories in their own right. That these inherited memories— traumatic fragments of events—defy narrative reconstruction.

Like so much else in our family story, scrambled birthdays seem to me one more detail, one more traumatic fragment of events that defy narrative reconstruction.

And yet piling fragment upon fragment is the best I can do, in the jars that line my mantel and in the story of my family, and it does add up to a picture that is something of a whole.

Like the recitation of names at a Yizkor service, a prayer for the departed, I am compelled to recite these fragments of my family history, to simply list the names, because sometimes that is the best we can do. There are no tombstones to mark the graves, so at least on these pages, the names reside.

There is my maternal great-grandmother Rose, or Reizel as she was called in Kolki, who would sometimes take my mother to Trochenbrod to visit her sister-in-law Sara Weinberg Bisker, who happened to be married to my father's cousin.

And my mother's older half sister, Lifsha, who was married to David Shuster. They met when he came from Trochenbrod to Kolki on business. Apparently, it was love at first sight. I have a number of pictures of Lifsha, with groups of friends, playing a balalaika, pictures with her husband and with one of their daughters, and a beautiful picture of her walking elegantly down the main street of Kolki with two of her aunts, her husband, David, her grandmother, and some cousins. "Shabbat walk in Kolki 1937" is written on the back of a photograph of a group of my female relatives, all of them wearing black, looking glamorous and carefree. If not for the inscription, I would have thought they were in Paris.

My mother's parents were Esther Weinberg and Srulach Bronstein, or Braunshtein, depending on who is doing the spelling. They were both widowed, their first spouses having died of tuberculosis.

My widowed grandmother Esther had a son in her first marriage who died and whose name I don't even know. My grandfather Srulach had a daughter, Lifsha, who became part of their new family.

Ethel, my mother, was the firstborn of my grandparents' second marriage. Her life was a new start for this fractured family.

Four years after my mother was born, Esther and Srulach had another daughter, Pesha—she of the shoes. Pesha was the quiet child, which is about the most I could get out of my mother, who almost never talked about her younger sister, other than to keep going back to the shoes.

My grandmother Esther came from a religious family that lived in a dorf, or village, called Kolikovich (Kulikowicze), near Kolki, along the Styr River. It had only a handful of families, and my grandmother's family may have been the only Jews.

My great-grandfather Yosef Weinberg was a tall, religious man, known for a fierce temper.

My great-grandmother Rose, or Reizel, was a tiny gentle woman, revered by her children and grandchildren. Like almost all of the Jews of Kolki, my great-grandparents and even my grandparents were related, either as cousins or through marriage.

My great-grandfather Yosef Weinberg's first cousin Itzak Sahm was married to my great-grandmother Rose's twin sister, Feiga.

Yosef and Rose's oldest daughter, Chia, sister of my grandmother Esther, married one of my grandfather Srulach's cousins. Two sisters married two cousins. And it goes on.

I wish I had more stories to attach to these names. A name is not a life, but sometimes it's the best we can do, and even in flattened form, this recitation is my way of merging memory with history.

One night recently, when I couldn't sleep, I went downstairs to my computer and started googling the name of the sanatorium in Poland where my maternal grandfather sought treatment and where he ultimately died. Remembering the name my mother had once mentioned, I tried several different spellings and finally stumbled on the TB sanatorium in Otwock, Poland, sixteen miles from Warsaw. The town apparently had a microclimate that made it a perfect place to treat patients with lung diseases. Isaac Bashevis Singer wrote about Otwock and its "crystal clear air." Following several links, I found the Otwock Jewish cemetery, which had a database of graves. One of those graves was that of "Israel Shlomo Bronstein, son of Natan Tzvi," whom we knew as Nissan. My grandfather's nickname was Srulach, although his given name was Israel. He died on March 14, 1927, and to my surprise, the website included an actual picture of his tombstone. I had a match! Now I had the exact date of his death and even my grandfather's middle name, Shlomo. I ran upstairs to tell Bert, who did not entirely share my enthusiasm in the middle of the night. My husband may be interested in my discoveries, but for him they can wait for sunrise.

As it happens, this is the only surviving tombstone of any of my immediate ancestors in all of Europe. Generations of my family lived in this part of the world, but all of their graves have either been destroyed or plowed over, or their bodies rest in mass graves, with no record of them anywhere other than in the Yad Vashem Holocaust database, if someone thought to enter their names.

My mother remained haunted all her life by the fact that she never said goodbye to her mother, who stood silently as she packed her things. She left without a plan. Just a winter coat, a pair of scissors, a change of clothes, and Pesha's shoes.

In the town square, she joined four of her girlfriends, Sura Kleiman, Bryna Weiman, Kittle Dricker, and Sura Mechlin. Together they followed the retreating Russian army and stayed ahead of the approaching Germans. But the five women were quickly separated in the chaos of their exodus. Three remained together and my mother ended up with Sura Mechlin, the one she knew least well. They spent the rest of the war as virtual sisters. All five of them survived and built new lives in Israel, Canada, and, in my mother's case, in the United States.

My mother and Sura traveled by horse-drawn wagon for a few days on the road east, with a Russian man my mother had worked with at a store in Kolki. But as the Soviet troops retreated, they saw the horse, wagon, and able-bodied young man and immediately requisitioned him. Before he left, however, he handed my mother a small suitcase and told her not to open it until he was gone. And here my mother did indeed have luck: The suitcase turned out to be filled with money that the man had taken from the store as he left. It was enough to get my mother and Sura started on their journey, even if it didn't last long.

The two "new sisters" kept moving east, following the retreating army, sleeping in barns and fields at night. They figured out how to hide stolen potatoes in the lining of their pants. People they met along the way sometimes gave them food. From the farmers, a little milk and maybe honey. Sometimes they just had to go hungry.

One difficult day's quest for survival led to another as they moved ever farther into Russia. They wandered the country for the ensuing three years, walking, hitching rides, sometimes hanging off trains. The grueling pace took a toll. My mother's legs swelled from all the walking. At one point, she developed sores from malnutrition, and Sura tended to her, sometimes helping her to dress. They became dependent on each other as they traveled, eventually making their way into Asia and figuring out how to survive moment to moment.

During the war, about one million Jews from the former Soviet Union, including Poland, managed to escape into Russia, with a significant number making it all the way into Central Asia, like my mother and Sura. It has been estimated that about 300,000 of these died due to disease and starvation, while others died as Soviet soldiers.

"I was the lucky one," my mother would say. "The others were in very, very bad shape, the ones I left behind."

My mother was the boss, Sura told me years later, when I first met her in Israel in 1999. Sura brought me a Kiddush cup, celebrating life, from her home as a gift to remember her by.

"If there were just ten grains of rice to put in water to make soup, Ethel insisted we save two for the next day," Sura said. They walked for miles, mostly by night, sometimes exchanging a little rice with local families for soap to wash themselves. My mother repeatedly told Sura that they had to save something so they could buy new dresses when they went home to see their families again.

They worked on farms and even in factories, making gun parts for the Soviet army. They found themselves in Kazakhstan and then, for a while, they worked in a city near Tashkent, Uzbekistan. The distance from Kolki to Tashkent is nearly 2,600 miles, if you use a direct route, about the same as the distance from New York to Los Angeles. Ethel and Sura hardly took a direct route, and much of the trip was on foot. But they were determined to make it, even as they watched people along the way giving up.

Sometime in 1944, when the war was not yet over, my mother and Sura heard that Kolki and neighboring shtetls had been liberated, so they immediately began to calculate how to go back home. They finally obtained a permit to leave Uzbekistan and go to the front lines in the west to offer medical support. Having survived this long, they had no interest in going to the front lines. Along the way they met a group of teenage Jewish girls who had become experts at forging documents and who produced falsified documents that would allow my mother and Sura to avoid the battles and go to Kolki.

They wrote a letter to Stalin—or at least he was the intended recipient—and somehow, somewhere, they received a letter from the Russian authorities saying all the Jews in Kolki had been killed. My mother and Sura refused to believe it. Even though the war wasn't actually over, they went home.

When they finally arrived in Kolki, they met Sura's brother-in-law, who had survived by hiding in the woods. He recounted everything that had happened to their families, person by person. After he told the handful of other returning survivors who returned to Kolki what had happened to their families, he left for Palestine, where, according to my mother, who met him years later, he literally never spoke another word.

———

I wish I knew more about him. I wish I had more details—my mother told me that she wished she'd had paper and pencil to record their journey, but she was too busy surviving. I can at least tell you what I know.

When they returned, my mother was able to identify her house—or her former house—which had been burned down; the wheel from the "oil factory" in the backyard was still there, sticking out of the ground.

As my mother wept, a woman on the other side of the street walked by, wearing her sister Lifsha's dress. There was no mistaking the dress, because it had been sent by an American relative.

My mother and Sura wanted to say Kaddish for their families, but the mass grave was in the forest outside the village, and they were warned against going into the woods.

A neighbor my mother knew, seeing that she and Sura were hungry, offered them a meal that included a piece of meat. Sura ate, but my mother wouldn't touch the meat. She recounted this story for Jonathan, when he was writing his book about vegetarianism, *Eating Animals*.

"He saved your life," Jonathan said.

"I didn't eat it."

"You didn't eat it?"

"It was pork. I wouldn't eat pork."

"Why?"

"What do you mean why?"

"What, because it wasn't kosher?"

"Of course."

"But not even to save your life?"

"If nothing matters, there's nothing to save."

3

My father's story proved more difficult to excavate. He died when I was eight, an event that is still difficult for me to talk about. Even as I have pieced together a plausible history, he remains an enigma; the more I learn, the less I know, both about him and his experience during the war.

There are no pictures of my father growing up, none of his prewar family, of his parents, who are my grandparents. No pictures of his sister and her husband, who are my aunt and uncle.

Bits and pieces of information have come together over the years from cousins in Israel and from other Trochenbrod survivors, in Brazil and Israel, from conversations in Ukraine, and from documents that only recently were made available through the Holocaust Museum. I have utilized every available ancestry tool I could find and have located long-lost relatives as well as ones I didn't know existed but none directly linked to my paternal grandfather's family. I have pieced together an impressive archive, but the reality is that it is easier to find information on—or at least references to—the fictitious shtetl that sprang from Jonathan's imagination than it is to find details about the place where my father actually lived.

I have come to accept that I will never know my father's full story: how he survived the war, the precise details of what he endured, of what haunted him and continued to cast shadows even on the new life he made in America. What I do know is that solving the mystery of the black-and-white photograph of my father and the family that hid him during the war, and of finding Trochenbrod—or at least assembling fragments of events, piecing together a narrative of the sister that I never knew—has been, for me, the way of finding my father.

I am writing today in my chilly basement office, wrapped in my Trochenbrod hoodie. It was given to Jonathan on the movie set of his adapted novel, which, were one to write a fairy-tale end to this tragic story, would pretty much sum up how strange and unexpected this journey for my father's past has proven to be.

"Memory begat memory begat memory," Jonathan writes of his fictitious "Trachimbrod," and it is in fact in these memories that my knowledge of the real Trochenbrod resides. Over the years, this search has led me to voraciously absorb every detail and anecdote that I can find, to assemble information about Trochenbrod piecemeal, like the shards of memory in my glass jars:

We know that after the rain fell, the air smelled like wildflowers.

That there was mud.

And geese.

And snakes.

And these snakes, according to one survivor, were so plentiful that they would come into the houses and the children would play with them and feed them at mealtimes, like pets. Once, a rabbi came to Trochenbrod and, hearing the complaints, said, "I will drive them away!" The rabbi went out into the field, tore up some grass, and threw it into the next field while uttering some words—a prayer, or a spell, or a shopping list, or a curse. Whatever it was, it worked, and that was the end of the snake infestation in Trochenbrod. Or so the story goes.

We know, from the interviews and memoirs of survivors, there were good solid houses, on high foundations, rectangular, with dirt floors.

A prosperous town, the population was 99 percent Jewish.

A thriving commercial center, it was *the* place to shop.

Some believe Sholem Aleichem visited Trochenbrod and drew inspiration there for his character Tevye the Dairyman.

The smell of freshly baked bread infused the air as the Sabbath approached, and in the summer, with the windows open, it might have been possible to hear everyone in town singing the same songs on the Sabbath, as though the village was one big family at one great meal.

The shtetl is gone and yet it still shapes my life. I have spent what seems like a lifetime gathering testimony from books and documentaries, from the few family photos that remain, from survivors' accounts, from oral histories, from reunions of survivors, and from the visit to Trochenbrod that I would undertake in 2009, with my son Frank. My home office overflows with papers and photographs, with large three-ring binders labeled "Trochenbrod," with boxes and folders full of documents and family stories. With map reproductions—some of such ancient provenance they look like they ought to be peopled by dragons and mythical beasts. With letters—tucked inside a folder, one of them five pages long, in neat, handwritten Yiddish from Itzhak Kimelblat in Brazil, eager to tell me his story, to maintain a connection to this vanished place.

While much of what I know about my family history has been deliberately and painstakingly assembled, a lifelong research project that has sent me on a scavenger hunt through libraries, the Internet, and around the globe, the broad outline of Trochenbrod's history requires no excavation—the arc of its inception to its violent decimation is readily accessible from the history books.

Trochenbrod was part of the Second Polish Republic before it was part of the Soviet Union before it was occupied by Nazi Germany as part of the Molotov–Ribbentrop Pact—or the German–Soviet Non-Aggression Pact or the Nazi German–Soviet Treaty of Non-Aggression, depending on which Wikipedia entry you prefer or where you stood in relation to the tanks.

Without getting too deep into the weeds of history, it is worth considering how it is that Jews wound up cultivating this marshy parcel of land, with its remote location, its poor soil, and its many snakes. Avrom Bendavid-Val, who was driven by a similar compulsion to explore Trochenbrod, notes in his book *The Heavens Are Empty* that Jews were not historically known as farmers, perhaps because of the conflict between religious practices and the demands of agrarian life—or maybe simply because of prohibitions against Jews owning land.

The short answer is that this part of Ukraine wound up, in the late 1700s, in what was known as Russia's Pale of Settlement, which stretched from the Baltic to the Black Sea and was home to between five and six million Jews.

It was in many ways idyllic and in more ways not. Jews were subject to heavy taxation, conscription into the Russian army, and were denied many civil rights. But they could avoid some of the more draconian measures if they agreed to cultivate farmland, which is what resulted in the creation of the Jewish shtetl of Trochenbrod.

These things I know from history books. What I have been able to gather from piecing together family history is more prosaic:

I know that my father's mother, Brucha, and her family lived in Trochenbrod, one house away from where her brother Yurchem and sister-in-law Sosel lived.

That a few houses farther up, on the same side of the road, were cousins Avrom and Sara Bisker.

That next door to them was Peretz Bisker, father of Ida Bisker Kogod, grandfather of Bob Kogod, whom we met in the United States. On the other side of the street were the Kimelblats, whose son Shai married my father's half sister, Choma.

I know that in Trochenbrod everyone had a nickname, something I learned later was important in identifying people. I would also learn that nicknames were derived from either a shortcoming or a profession. Accordingly, there was Chaim Nutta, the shoemaker. And Shaul Avramchick, who was known as the big eater; "Belly Button" Itzy, who was a government-appointed rabbi. There was Leib "the big one" and Leib "the small one." There was Itzy "with the nose" and Helchick the butcher and Ephraim "who cries in the synagogue" and Pinchas the carpenter and Yankel the blacksmith and Chava the midwife and Ydel "the dumb one," and I could go on and on, and perhaps I should, because part of the point of this narrative is to keep these stories alive.

Despite my efforts, it remains the case that I know virtually nothing about the Safran side, my paternal grandfather's family. I don't know whether my grandfather had any siblings or where he came from. I hired a researcher in Ukraine in 2005 to try to find documents that might shed light on my grandfather's family. He found nothing and believes my grandfather Yosef Safran came from elsewhere, probably a larger town. The only record that I could find is a 1929 Polish business directory available on the Internet, which lists a "Szafran" doing business in Trochenbrod.

Actually, I learned years later that my grandmother's family, the Biskers, didn't exactly come from Trochenbrod but from its adjacent sister village, called Lozisht. The two were connected, along a single road, and always thought of together.

While my father had some distant cousins in the United States, none of them knew him before he immigrated. His closest relatives were three first cousins living in Israel. From them I learned that my grandmother Brucha remarried and my father had a half sister, Choma or Nechoma. My father's cousin Shmuel Bisker told me that my father was not only his cousin but his best friend.

I know that, according to Shmuel, my father was the best student for miles around and that he always had "a head for business."

I know, from my mother, that my father was always running: building a business, going from one store to the next. In the end, maybe there was finally no more running left in him.

I know, from reflection, that outlasting the war didn't necessarily mean surviving.

There is only one picture of my father taken before my parents met: It's the black-and-white photo of him, another man, and two women. My mother told me that she met the other man in the photograph twice, when he came to see my father in Lutsk. She remembers my father taking great care of the man, and she thinks the man was always smiling—in her mind this was because he was proud that he had helped to save my father. She said the man came to Lutsk because he wanted my father to return to their village to live and to marry his daughter.

When I asked my mother why she didn't know more or ask questions, she said that after the war people didn't want to talk about the past. This must have been especially true when survivors, like my father, remarried and started new families. They wanted to move on and focus on building new lives. Then, when they came to the United States, no one asked questions. American relatives were either afraid to ask or afraid to hear what had happened in Europe. Maybe they didn't know how to ask. Or maybe they felt guilty for not having done more to help their families.

And yet, after the passage of all this time, there is a need to remember, to take whatever fragments I can find and piece together a vanished shtetl where the living quarters and the stables for the horses and cattle were sometimes one and the same, and where the chickens were kept behind the stove, and the potatoes under the bed, and in the winter, during the heavy freeze, the calves were kept inside the house. Where there were not only snakes but a flame. And every evening the flame could be seen glowing near the forest. Sometimes the flame would be large and sometimes small. Sometimes it would appear low down near the ground, and at other times it would leap high. As with the snakes, the people in Trochenbrod grew accustomed to it. When a person went up close to take a look at the flame, it disappeared. Whether or not there really was such a flame, or the snakes were pets, or Trochenbrod was an inspiration for Sholem Aleichem, this vanished shtetl was so colorful, so magically rendered by its former inhabitants, that it's no wonder my son Jonathan turned it into a work of fiction.

We know there was a strong work ethic and fertile soil in Trochenbrod.

There were dairy farms, leather factories, a glass factory, retail shops, school buildings, synagogues.

The children who grew up in Trochenbrod were strong and healthy—a "Trochenbrod boy," it was said, "could knock out ten peasants!"

There was only one Christian family—under Polish law, the postmaster could not be Jewish.

Jewish families from neighboring villages sent their girls to Trochenbrod for fattening before marriage.

The entire town came out to celebrate weddings.

Gentile women came from nearby villages to milk the cows on the Sabbath.

The town had one main, unpaved road, running through Trochenbrod and up through Lozisht. It was lined by bollards meant to prevent the horses from slipping into the drainage ditches alongside the thoroughfare.

Menorahs for Chanukah were crafted from halved potatoes (the ones, perhaps, that were kept under the bed) into which a small hole would be made, and oil poured, and a piece of cotton lit.

Behind each house was farmland, behind which was forest.

There was no electricity.

Mud bears repeating twice.

When the Germans arrived in 1941, the Trochenbroders did not, at first, panic. They had lived under German rule before, and in fact many remembered that, during World War I, the Germans served as quasi-protectors from the Russians.

We know that even if the people of Trochenbrod did sense that something was about to happen, the way that my mother knew, a certain stasis may have set in. It is easy, with hindsight, to sense that one should flee, but when I try to imagine myself in that situation, I understand how hard it would be to leave behind everything I had ever known. To simply walk away from your life, your friends, your home, your few possessions.

Besides, there was the possibility that some of the stories circulating at the time, about what had happened to others, were perhaps not true. Or maybe they were true, but whatever had happened to them couldn't possibly happen again.

This is why the people of Trochenbrod were later referred to as *luftmenschen,* which translates to "airmen" or to "one who is not a realist," because they did not believe the truth.

Some of the Jews were employed by the Germans to police their own, and they were called *Judenrat.*

The Ukrainians from neighboring villages were encouraged to rampage.

On August 9, 1942, twenty men from a German extermination unit arrived: *Einsatzgruppe C.*

There were eleven army trucks.

The Jews were ordered to the center of town. This included Trochenbroders and Jews from eastern Poland who were escaping the Nazis.

They were told to line up and to put a hand on the shoulder of the person in front of them.

The Germans took pictures and measured the length and width of these people standing in line, the Jewish population, so that they could then use those measurements to calculate the depth and width of the necessary graves.

But the calculations would not be entirely accurate, because some of these Jews were shot, randomly, along the way.

They were told they would now relocate to a ghetto.

On August 11, people were taken two hundred at a time to the pit and shot in what is known as the first "Aktion."

Five hundred to one thousand people remained alive.

Some of them fled into the forest. But then, on Yom Kippur, September 21, many of them emerged from the woods, hungry and frozen, to celebrate Yom Kippur together, and the Germans were waiting.

By the time this was over, roughly sixty Jews were left.

Germans worked the land for a while, after the Jews were gone, until the Jewish partisans, who were resistance fighters, came back and destroyed some of the village.

We know from Israelis born in Trochenbrod that, after that, the Soviets destroyed the rest of what remained. The Soviets wanted to erase physical evidence of a Jewish settlement, so they carried off any remnants and incorporated the land into a kolkhoz, a Soviet collective farm, ironically named "New Life."

What I know about how my father managed to escape the massacre of his ghetto is largely because of his cousin. Ida Bisker Kogod, meeting my father for the first time in the United States, dared to ask him how he survived. He told her that he and a friend, another Jew in their ghetto, were sent by the Nazis on a work detail to repair windows in a train station some distance away. It was during that time that the Nazis decided to liquidate the ghetto in Chetvertnia, where he and his family had been taken. When my father and his friend returned, a Ukrainian with a horse and wagon told him that everyone had been massacred. According to my mother, my father said that his first instinct was to turn himself in and die with the rest of his family. The Ukrainian, as the story goes, told him he could do that later, but meanwhile he hid him in his wagon and covered him with straw. He allowed my father to stay with him for only one night, afraid that if my father was found in his house, the Ukrainian farmer and his family would be murdered.

I don't know where my father was during most of the war. One former Trochenbroder told me that he is sure he went east, all the way to Moscow. I can't imagine how that is possible and I will probably never know. What I do know is that at least at the end of the war he was hiding in the home of a neighbor, the one in the picture that my mother managed to save. He survived because one righteous person risked his life and those of his wife and children by letting my father hide in the barn behind his house. I don't know for how long or when during the time of the German occupation he hid there. The man's children stood guard outside, taking turns pretending to play as a way to keep watch for any approaching Germans. Fortunately, after the exterminations, the Germans entered the village only intermittently.

The picture has some scribbling on the back. Over the years, we tried to make sense of it but couldn't. The one word that we could make out was something like "Augustine," which we thought might be part of an address. Maybe it was a town. Or a street. Or a person.

This was the photograph that Jonathan took with him, years later, as he left for the trip to Trochenbrod that gave rise to *Everything Is Illuminated*. He had set out to find Augustine.

4

In the wedding photograph, such as it is, my father wears an elegant dark suit and a crisp white shirt. His tie is striped, and what appears to be a new fedora sits atop his head. The camera has caught him with his eyes half open, which is halfway more than my mother's, closed beneath the white veil that obscures her face.

Were they thinking about the past with those hooded eyes or conjuring some better future? Who can say? What is evident from this photo, however, is my mother's trademark superstition. Something, or someone, has been disappeared— literally cut out of the picture. It's no neat job, this erasure. Unlike the discreet photoshopped removals of today, this one more closely resembles a decapitation. When I asked my mother who this was, she explained that two weddings took place that day, one right after the other, which was bad luck. Presumably she meant the other couple had been excised from this photograph, but it's really hard to tell, because there are two other random people visible here, as well as a pair of hands.

I have one other picture that looks like it was taken either right before or right after the wedding. My father is in the same suit and tie. My mother and father look so happy, close to each other, with their heads pressed together. My mother, with her hair pulled back, is wearing a beautiful dress with a large brooch. It is my favorite picture of my parents, and this is how I like to think of them, looking radiant, even if their happiness was brief.

My parents on their wedding day.

At least I have these mementos, along with the tattered ketubah, a Jewish wedding contract, mended over the years with now-yellowing tape. This I found tucked inside my mother's sturdy secret cardboard box, carefully covered with decorative Con-Tact paper and always hidden in the back of a closet until I was able to retrieve it many years later. Part of the ketubah is missing, torn neatly along the seam, but unlike the deliberate doctoring of the photograph, this missing part appears to be unintended, just an unfortunate consequence of age. The ketubah is quite large and decorative, preprinted with blanks to fill in.

My parents married in Lodz, about seventy-five miles southwest of Warsaw, on May 5, 1945, according to DP-camp documents that I found. They had known each other only a few months, after meeting in Lutsk, in western Ukraine—the largest city in the vicinity of their respective shtetls and a gathering place for Jewish survivors. By the standards of the time, they were practically an old couple. Quick marriages were typical among refugees. Some couples married after meeting only weeks before, according to my mother. "Life wasn't normal," she explained. There was no time to worry about normal, whatever that meant or had once meant. These were people who had lost everything and everyone—entirely, tragically, literally. They were eager to begin life again, to start families, or new families. To close their eyes and commit to life.

I was talking with a friend whose parents were also married in Poland at around the same time. When I told him that my parents were married on May 5, he looked right at me and said, "No, they weren't." How did he know? He said his parents were married in another Polish city on May 1 and that I needed to check the ketubah carefully. He was right. May 5 was a Saturday, the Jewish Sabbath, a time when weddings are not performed, except after sundown. The ketubah has the Hebrew date of the eighteenth day of the month of Iyar, which is the Jewish holiday of Lag B'Omer, the same holiday on which my mother says she was born. Omer is a forty-nine-day somber period between the festivals of Passover and Shavuot; the origins of the holiday are unclear. But we do know that the thirty-third day of this period, Lag B'Omer, offers a break from the mourning and is the one day during this period when Jewish weddings are permitted.

Jews desperate to start new lives, whatever they may have believed after what they had been through, were waiting for the thirty-third day, for an official Jewish wedding. It is the day my parents got married and the day my friend's parents got married along with many other Jewish refugee couples. In 1945 Lag B'Omer was on May 1. Interestingly, this was the day after Hitler committed suicide. Just a few days later, on May 7, the Germans surrendered, ending the war in Europe.

Lodz, where my parents married and where I was born, was the second-largest Jewish community in prewar Poland, after Warsaw. Warsaw was totally destroyed in the war. Lodz, however, survived German occupation with relatively little physical damage. One-third of Lodz's population had been Jewish prior to the war. Of the approximately 233,000 Jews in Lodz at that time, about 200,000 were forced to live in the city's ghetto, and it is estimated that somewhere between only 5,000 and 7,000 Jews from the ghetto survived. By 1946 the number had swelled to about 50,000 Jews, most from elsewhere in Europe, who saw it as a waystation and crossroads from the east as they tried to escape a Europe that clearly did not want them.

My parents lived in an apartment in Lodz that had once been occupied by a murdered Jewish family; the city was full of empty homes and businesses that had previously belonged to Jews.

They shared their first apartment with another Jewish refugee couple, who were also expecting a baby. Whoever managed the doling out of these vacant apartments must have figured this was a good match: Both women were expecting their first child, without any family members to help, so they would presumably benefit from mutual support.

The couples agreed that the first mother to give birth would get the best bedroom and the other mother would help take care of the new family and cook for them. Then they would change places when the next baby was born.

There is no official record that I have been able to find of my arrival in a Lodz hospital on March 17, 1946. I slid into the world right under the iron curtain. Days before I was born, on March 5, 1946, Winston Churchill gave one of his most famous speeches, at Westminster College in Fulton, Missouri, announcing ". . . an iron curtain has descended across the Continent. Behind that line lie all the capitals of the ancient states of Central and Eastern Europe . . . and all are subject, in one form or another, not only to Soviet influence but to a very high and in some cases increasing measure of control from Moscow."

A researcher that I hired to find my birth certificate was unable to locate any documents. Apparently, at that time in Poland, births were not automatically recorded. My parents would have had to make an effort to register the birth, and it's possible that they had seen enough to know that being on any official registry at this moment in history would be unlikely to do me any good.

"Everything is going to be good" was the gist of the messages delivered to my mother while she lay on a bed in the hallway of the hospital, alone, unanesthetized, and ready to give birth to her first child, although I would later learn that I was not my father's first child. My father was not allowed to be with her during her very long labor, but at least he managed to send encouraging notes.

Esther Brucha Safran. I was named for my two murdered grandmothers: my mother's mother, Esther Weinberg Bronstein, and my father's mother, Brucha Bisker Safran Kuperschmit. By coincidence it was also Purim, the celebration of Queen Esther, the unexpected queen of ancient Persia, who saved the Jews.

My name may have been intended to keep the memory of my grandmothers alive, but I seemed to intuitively understand from the beginning that my role was to bring joy. To point my family toward a brighter future while carrying with me the names of two murdered grandmothers. Whether I succeeded I can't say with certainty, but I have tried.

It must have seemed a miracle to my father—a baby girl, alive, with a chest that could rise and fall, after his first daughter, the one he never spoke of to me, was murdered.

Time must have stood still for a little while as we waited in this apartment, the former owners now ghosts. As we went about the business of living, breathing new life into the chunky prewar furniture—the chairs that others had once sat in, the table they had eaten at, the beds they had slept in. We were a long way from the dirt roads of Kolki and Trochenbrod, but we still had a long way to go.

There's a photograph of my parents on the street somewhere in Lodz: My mother is wearing a hat, her arm linked through my father's arm, and another man on the other side.

They all look chic in their tall boots, and I like to imagine that this was a happy interregnum, that they were jaunty and carefree, enjoying this more cosmopolitan life, even though I know it was not. Their smiles belie the horrors they have just been through, not to mention that they were surely overwhelmed by such adult concerns as making a living, putting food on the table, getting this family to a better place.

Over the years I pressed my mother for more details about Lodz, but unsurprisingly most of what she remembered had to do with being a new young mother who did not have her own mother to guide her.

Eventually she opened up, and what she told me proved far more colorful than I would have thought. At first she said something about a deli. But then, when pressed, she wasn't confident it was really a deli. I would later learn that although there was in fact an establishment that served food and drink, it may have been something of a front, that the money came from money itself. My parents changed currency and they bought gold that had been melted down for easy transport. They did this for the largely transient population that was moving from east to west in search of a future.

The deli, such as it was, gave free drinks to local police and other authorities, I discovered from one of my father's partners, to keep local officials lubricated and on their side. And the business that propped up the business was so successful that my father and his partners had a Jewish cobbler carve out the heels of old shoes as a hiding place for money and valuables. They used old shoes only so as to be less conspicuous—they didn't want to draw attention with any suggestion of prosperity. I often wonder if this made my mother think of Pesha's shoes.

I learned most of this from Itzhak Kimelblat, whom I met several times in Rio and whom Frank was able to interview separately on a couple of trips to Brazil. The Kimelblats came from Trochenbrod, or actually from Lozisht, our particular "suburb" of Trochenbrod. The map of the shtetl shows them living across the road from my grandmother Brucha's house. Itzhak told me that he went to school with Choma, my father's half sister, and that Choma married Itzhak's cousin Shai Kimelblat, which made us almost family.

When I first met him in Rio, Itzhak was nearly ninety, fit, stylish, and equipped with a phenomenal memory. I asked him about the business the Kimelblats shared with my father and several other partners, and he said nonchalantly, "Oh, you mean at Seventy-eight Piotrkowska Street?" I searched for the address online—and there it was: the street and the building. I recognized it immediately as the backdrop of pictures of my parents along with their business partners, including Itzhak Kimelblat and his brother, Natan. It's an elegant old building, with beautiful architecture, located on one of the most magnificent streets in Lodz. Today the street is bustling with cafés and bookstores and shops.

I also learned that this had been the 1887 birthplace of the pianist Arthur Rubinstein. Today there is a plaque on the building and, outside it, a life-size bronze figure of Rubinstein seated at a grand piano.

Across the street, at 77 Piotrkowska, is a former mansion and bank that once belonged to another successful Lodz Jew, the banker Maksymilian Goldfeder. Now it has been transformed into a club. The street is lined with mansions, banks, and textile factories that were once owned by other murdered Jewish industrialists. At one point, the largest building in the heart of Lodz was the "Great" Synagogue, which was burned down by the Nazis in 1939, along with the rest of the synagogues. There's another chilling reminder of the city's history: During World War II, the street was briefly renamed Adolf Hitler Strasse.

The business my father and his partners created required quick thinking; they had to memorize fluctuating exchange rates and be able to convert currencies without the aid of calculators. These guys from Trochenbrod may not have had much education, but they were shrewd. I sometimes thought of this as I watched my mother holding up the line at the CVS register, counting her coupons, running the numbers through her head to make sure there wasn't a mistake.

Given my mother's wartime heroics, her cross-continental journey made largely on foot, and her ability to intuit the dangers ahead, it's not hard to imagine her as a successful associate in the family's shadow trade. She told me she once traveled to Kiev with gold coins strapped clandestinely around her waist. My father told her where to go, gave her the address and the names of the contacts. I'm not sure if she was trading currency for gold or vice versa. She had one close call on the train, when a man tried to pick her up. She was terrified that his advances might lead to him touching her and finding the secret belt of gold, but she managed to extricate herself somehow. Anyway, mission accomplished. I assume this took place before I was born and that after I arrived she gave up these sorts of gutsy missions, but, knowing her, I can't say for sure.

From what I now know about our time in Lodz, my parents engaged in their deli–cum–currency franchise for about a year and a half. And even though Itzhak helped fill in many details of this period, he and Natan were in business with my father for only a few months. There were other partners who came and went, as evidenced by the pictures outside the deli where my father poses with a changing cast of characters. In one photograph, Itzhak and Natan wear the war medals they received for fighting as partisans, Itzhak still nursing war injuries that have him leaning on a cane.

Other landsmen came through Lodz, looking for whatever family they could find, including my father's first cousin Gadia Bisker. When I met Gadia in Israel many years later, he bragged that he had been my first babysitter. My parents helped him get back on his feet, bought him new clothes and shoes, but apparently he was not all that eager to find real work, much to my father's frustration. It's not hard to imagine how he might have lost his will. He was the only one of my father's cousins to survive the massacres in Trochenbrod. Gadia's sisters and their families, as well as his mother, were all killed, probably alongside my own grandmother and Aunt Choma.

Two of Gadia's brothers had left before the war. Shmuel and Yehoshua Bisker were among the Zionists from Trochenbrod who went to Palestine in the mid-1930s, and Gadia was focused on getting out of Poland to join them, which he did, eventually. After the war, more than 70,000 Jews arrived illegally in British Palestine on more than one hundred ships that picked up refugees who had moved through Europe by foot or in disguised vehicles to ports along the Mediterranean Sea. Not everyone made it: Many more refugees were stopped by British patrols and sent to internment camps in Cyprus.

My parents may have managed to begin a family, to run a business, to wear fashionable-looking boots, but there were constant reminders that this was not where they were meant to stay. Between 1944 and 1946 there were a series of anti-Semitic incidents in Poland, occurring at a time of general lawlessness and civil war against the Soviet-backed Communists. And, it was increasingly clear that the "iron curtain" was going to make it difficult to leave. Itzhak said that a young girl sent by Brihah (which literally means "to escape" and was the name of an organization that worked to get Jewish refugees across closed borders from Europe to Palestine) came to their store one day and told them it was time to get out of Poland.

Itzhak and Natan, both young and unencumbered, made their way through Europe to Italy and ultimately to Rio, where they had relatives. Once in Brazil, Natan began life as a peddler and went on to build one of the largest jewelry chains in the country, launching a brand of watches bearing his name. My husband, Bert, still proudly wears his Natan watch today. In fact, Natan arrived in the country shortly after two other Jewish immigrant jewelers—Hans Stern and Jules Roger Sauer—who were also fleeing persecution; all three built major international brands.

We stayed in Lodz a little longer. Escaping for us was complicated because I was a baby. But there were constant reminders that we needed to leave, including individual assaults and pogroms, such as the one in Kielce, on July 4, 1946, where forty-two Jews were murdered and many more injured. It was time to get out.

When I was close to six months old, in August or September 1946, we finally left Lodz. We had to employ some spycraft to slip away undetected. My mother traveled light, packing only a few things, and told her neighbors that she and I were going away for a few days. My father went to work as usual. At some point during the day, my father said that he was going out for a break, or maybe he said he was running an errand. He never returned.

They met up at a designated location, where they had arranged transport from the middle of Poland to the middle of Germany and then to a displaced-persons camp in the American zone. My mother remembered a covered truck with a false bottom, which was where we hid for part of the journey. Among the things she packed were some small silver Kiddush cups, called *becher* in Yiddish, but along the way she started throwing them out, afraid of being caught with them if we were stopped. Knowing what I know now, I'm sure there was money or gold stuffed into the heels of shoes or in the linings of their clothing, and possibly other valuables hidden, as well—all easier to disguise than bulky silver cups.

The biggest challenge, my mother said, was traveling with a baby. She had to stuff cloth into my mouth to keep me quiet as we made our way through dangerous territory. We traveled this way from Lodz to Berlin, which on a direct route was about three hundred miles. Today, on good roads in a modern vehicle, the trip would take about five hours, so I can only imagine how long and harrowing our journey was. My mother recalled few details, apart from how awful she felt having to gag her child. It's probably just as well that she couldn't remember more; surely these were not memories to preserve—apart from that we made it.

5

You see what you want to see, or maybe what you need to see, in a photograph, and for much of my life I would look at the pictures from the almost three years we spent in Germany and see all the signs of a normal family life. There I am, mugging for the camera, perched on my tricycle. And in another photo, looking adorably overwhelmed in my too-big, fluffy white rabbit-hooded coat. And there are my parents, fashionably dressed again, surrounded by friends, seated at an outdoor picnic. To see them you might think they are at a backyard barbecue, characters in a Cheever story, masking their suburban ennui with smiles.

Look closer. In the background there are watchtowers, run-down barracks, and a barbed-wire fence. We were exiles. Stateless. People without a country. In Hebrew, we were *She'arit Hapleta*—the surviving remnant. We were displaced persons, and, accordingly, we were assigned to live in a displaced-persons camp.

The DP camps, where most Jewish refugees ended up after the war, are often a forgotten epilogue. The very existence of these camps is referenced only in passing, if at all, in

My parents, with me in a stroller, walking through a displaced-persons camp.

the otherwise vast body of Holocaust literature, even though nearly 300,000 Jewish survivors passed through these camps in Germany from 1945 to 1950. Scholar Margarete Myers Feinstein, in her 2010 book, *Holocaust Survivors in Postwar Germany, 1945–1957,* shares an amusing anecdote about this frequent omission: At the end of the film *Schindler's List,* a Soviet officer arrives on horseback at the gates of a labor camp and tells the surviving Jews they are free to go. The film then fast-forwards some fifty years; the liberated Jews are now seen striding across the hills in Israel. But what happened to them in between?

By the summer of 1945, Jews who had survived concentration camps, or had managed to hide, or had joined up with the partisans, or had survived in the Soviet Union, began arriving in Germany, viewing it as a stop on the way to a better life. The Allied plan was to repatriate the refugees to their home countries. For Jewish refugees, though, this wasn't an option; not only were their homes gone and their families murdered, but in many cases the local population—their former friends and neighbors—had aided in their persecution. Understandably, they refused to go back, and no other countries wanted them. Palestine was closed to legal immigration at that time, and even the United States had immigration quotas that favored non-Jews. Virtually every option for emigration out of the graveyard of Europe was closed.

Hundreds of DP camps were established, not just in Germany but also in Austria and Italy, and they housed some 850,000 people that, in addition to Jews, included Armenians, Poles, Latvians, Lithuanians, Estonians, Greeks, Russians, Ukrainians, as well as others.

Accommodations were largely improvised. On one end of the spectrum, a DP camp was set up in a castle; at the other end, in a former concentration camp.

Any available edifice had to do, including children's summer camps, concentration camps, hospitals, private homes, and army barracks or POW camps.

Camps were often filthy, reflecting poor preparation by the Allies, plain negligence, or, in more than a few cases, outright contempt for the Jewish refugees. Basic necessities such as underwear, shoes, toilet paper, and toothbrushes were in short supply. Some refugees still wore striped pajamas from the concentration camps, and—just as horrifying—others were given German SS uniforms to wear. There were reports that refugees were provided with less food per day than German prisoners of war had received.

The war may have been over, but that didn't mean sentiments had entirely changed. In some camps, German police, some of them ex-Nazis, were put in charge. There were reports of anti-Semitism among some of the American soldiers stationed at the DP camps, as well. Not to mention their DP-camp cohabitants—in the beginning, some Jewish refugees were living beside the same Poles, Lithuanians, Latvians, and others who had collaborated with the Nazis.

Two Jewish U.S. Army privates who were stationed in Germany in 1945, Edward Herman and Robert Hilliard, discovered the terrible treatment of a group of Jewish DPs at St. Ottilien, a camp run in the American zone by the U.S. military. Hilliard ultimately wrote a book about their experiences, titled, appropriately, *Surviving the Americans*. In Bavaria, St. Ottilien was the site of a hospital that was set up by the survivors themselves—a group that included several doctors who had been prisoners in concentration camps—because no medical facilities were being provided by the U.S. military at that time. Thousands of Jews were still dying from weakness and disease and were not able to find any medical help, other than from fellow Jewish survivors.

These two young GIs smuggled whatever food they could carry, such as powdered milk and eggs, from their mess hall to the nearby hospital DP camp, where they found sick and emaciated patients who were not getting any attention. They recruited other GIs to help smuggle the food past the American military police, who were under orders not to let unofficial supplies in. Despite the American presence, the local civilian governments often had the same people in control as had been under the Nazis.

In frustration, these American Jewish privates crafted a nine-page letter describing the horrors of what they were witnessing and accusing the American people of genocide. "By your unconcerned neglect," they wrote, "you are just as responsible for the present death of the European Jews as the most diabolical of Nazis was in the past. No, you scream! Well, yes, we scream, as do thousands of Jews in Europe who are today destitute, without food, shelter, clothing, or medical aid."

They sent copies of the letter to anyone they could think of who might be able to help and asked recipients to forward the letter to others, especially to influential political leaders and Jewish organizations.

One of their letters, it was reported, eventually reached President Harry Truman, who had already asked Earl G. Harrison, head of the University of Pennsylvania Law School and a former commissioner of immigration, to personally investigate the conditions of the DP camps. Truman asked Harrison to also look into the charges in the letter and to check out these two GIs, to understand their background and possible motives. Harrison even visited Hilliard's mother. They must have passed muster.

Harrison reported back on August 1, 1945, that conditions were so grim that "we appear to be treating the Jews as the Nazis treated them, except that we do not exterminate them."

This led to a front-page article in *The New York Times* on September 30, 1945, under the headline PRESIDENT ORDERS EISENHOWER TO END NEW ABUSE OF JEWS.

The worst situation was reported to have developed in southern Germany in the camps under General George Patton. Patton wrote in his diary that he believed the Jewish DPs were "a subhuman species without any of the cultural or social refinements of our times." Patton was relieved of his command by General Eisenhower, and President Truman appointed an adviser to the military with sole responsibility for the camps. Jewish chaplains were also important in prodding the military to treat the refugees more humanely, as was pressure from relief workers. It all took time—too much time—but conditions began to improve.

From what I can piece together, our family made its way from Lodz to a camp in Berlin, where we must have been for just a short time. Then, as some camps closed and others opened to accommodate the large number of people flowing west, we moved a couple of times before winding up in a former military barracks in Ziegenhain.

Ziegenhain is a beautiful medieval town, which included a camp built by the Nazis to house their POWs. François Mitterrand, who was later president of France, was among the early inhabitants.

By 1945, Stalag IX-A Ziegenhain's population included more than a thousand American POWs, many of whom were captured at the Battle of the Bulge in late 1944. Jewish POWs were routinely singled out by the Germans, and many of them were sent to labor camps. But there are stories of heroics. In January 1945, the Germans announced that all Jewish POWs were to report the following morning. The highest-ranking American at the POW camp, Master Sergeant Roddie Edmonds, who had been a prisoner for about one hundred days, ordered *all* of the Americans—Jews and non-Jews—to report and stand together. There were more than one thousand Americans standing in wide formation in front of the barracks, with Sergeant Edmonds positioned in front.

"We are all Jews," Edmonds told the German officer in charge. The German took out his pistol and pointed it at Edmonds. Edmonds refused to give in. "If you shoot me, you will have to shoot all of us, and after the war you will be tried for war crimes." Remarkably, this worked: The German officer walked away.

After the POW camp had been liberated in March 1945, Stalag IX-A Ziegenhain became Internment Camp 95 and was used by the U.S. Army to hold Nazi soldiers until mid-1946.

Then it was our turn. Beginning in August 1946, the filthy POW barracks of Stalag IX-A and Internment Camp 95 became DP Camp 95-443 Ziegenhain—our new home. My guess is that we must have arrived right about the time the POW camp became a DP camp, because my birth certificate—the falsified one, the only one—indicates that by September 8 of that year we were there.

In 1933, the town had only fifty-three Jews. Now there were thousands of Jews, including about two thousand in our camp.

Ziegenhain is the backdrop for my earliest memories. Or perhaps these are my earliest memories because I have so many photographs and have heard so many stories about this time and place. I was, as I suppose I should have been, oblivious to the narrative that had brought us here, accepting of our conditions, focused on my family and my many new friends, my white rabbit coat, and my tricycle. In these photographs, I look happy and beloved—and I surely am.

Riding my tricycle around the displaced-persons camp.

Ziegenhain is also close to my heart because of my fictitious birth here, and when I see the photographs of my birthday parties at the camp, I can't help but wonder which of the
dates my parents chose to celebrate.

There wasn't any privacy in the old barracks where we
lived. Bathrooms and kitchens were shared, and there were
holes in the wall between our space and the one next door.
Before going to bed—in a military cot, as there were no cribs
when we first arrived—I would peek through the wall and
wish our neighbors *a gute nakht*, "a good night" in Yiddish.
These neighbors were my parents' closest friends in the DP
camp: Ruchel and Aaron Brenner. At least one benefit of this

sort of communal living is that close, lifelong friendships were forged. Aaron was my father's business partner in the DP camp, and Ruchel was my mother's closest friend. Mine, too: In many of the photographs, I can be seen walking between Ruchel and my mother, holding both of their hands. In other photos, it is just Ruchel and me, arm in arm.

In the beginning, food, clothing, and medicine were in short supply. Instead of being able to go to the local markets to buy fresh produce and meat, which the local Germans could do, my mother got packaged food from the American military and Jewish agencies. There were things she had never seen before. In one disbursement, there were boxes of a packaged powdery substance. My mother stared at it in confusion. Brightly colored, it tasted sweet. Apparently this food item was called Jell-O. She had no idea what she was meant to do with it.

The definition of normal life is elastic, and even under these difficult conditions, vibrant makeshift communities emerged. There were DP schools and theaters and even newspapers. There were also many marriages and, unsurprisingly, numerous births—a reflection of the fact that most of the survivors were in their twenties, the older and younger generations being less likely to have made it through the war alive. These young refugees wanted to start over, and the most affirming way to defy Hitler's attempt to exterminate the Jews was with new life—and new life was everywhere. The DP camps had the highest birth rate of any place in the world at that time.

My life also had a certain normalcy to it because my father—he of the shoes with hollow heels—was a shrewd businessman who knew how to make a buck. He didn't want to live like a prisoner. He wasn't one to sit around and wait for handouts, so he turned to the black market. For some of the DPs, this was a way to simply get better food and clothing. For others, like my father and his four partners—one of whom was Aaron, our neighbor through the hole in the wall—it was a way to accumulate portable wealth for use when they were finally resettled. The partners traded everything: food, cigarettes, jewelry, coffee, and chocolate, all of which were in short supply. My mother remembered large trucks pulling right up to the camp to deliver supplies for their black-market business. Needless to say, this all went on much to the annoyance of the American military, yet somehow or other, shady commerce thrived.

Years later, in Israel, I would visit Ruchel and Aaron and learn more about our time in the camp. They told me that on one occasion, Aaron and my father had some black-market goods—gold or jewelry—laid out on one of the cots. We were all in the common space when a soldier arrived unexpectedly to do an inspection. According to Aaron, I was an eager partner in crime: I went back into the room with the cot, took the goods off the bed, and hid them underneath. Nothing was discovered. My mother didn't remember this, but I choose to believe that it is true.

It was only recently, in talking about this with my children and watching my grandchildren, that I was able to appreciate the emotional complexity of this act. Even as a child I was eager to oblige and understood that my role was to bring joy, even when that meant being complicit in breaking the rules.

Sometimes I wonder how my parents must have felt, giving up what seemed like a reasonably good, cosmopolitan life in Lodz, with a nice apartment and the freedom to come and go, for what would become almost three relatively difficult years, with an uncertain future and life on hold. That said, I suspect that my father's business savvy likely enabled us to enjoy more comforts than most of our fellow DPs. It seemed to me that I had plenty at the time—that tricycle was certainly the envy of my playmates. I had my own little toddler-sized leather suitcase, black with brown leather trim. I carried it proudly when we later traveled across the Atlantic. Now a bit battered, that suitcase is still one of my most prized possessions.

Cash did not solve every problem, of course. I had several health scares while we were in Germany, including a handful of asthma attacks—a condition now shared by two of my grandchildren. I sometimes wonder how I survived what can be life-threatening attacks. It wasn't simply that the remedies available at the time were probably unsophisticated, but medical care in postwar Germany involved German doctors, of whom Jewish DPs were often rightfully suspicious. On one occasion when my parents took me to a clinic for my breathing difficulties, they were told they would have to leave me there overnight, alone. My parents refused. On another occasion, my mother took me to a doctor who demonstrated his inner Nazi by telling her to slap me when I was crying, so that I would shut up. We left quickly. My friend Gina Roitman, born in a different DP camp, in Passau, Germany, produced a 2013 documentary about a Nazi midwife who deliberately killed Jewish newborns by pressing down on their fontanels. The mothers were told their babies died naturally during childbirth. When the American military began to realize that an alarming number of babies were dying, they exhumed the bodies to conduct autopsies. They wound up prosecuting the

Nazi midwife, but by then she had killed more than fifty Jewish babies—and this after the war had ended.

According to my mother, I never crawled. Instead, at the age of nine months, I simply stood up and walked. Considering the physical conditions of the camp, I can imagine why no one would put a child down on the floor to crawl. There's an easy analogy to be made here: If you wanted to survive, you had to pick yourself up.

Walking came with its own set of dangers. Once, I was playing with another toddler in the communal kitchen while someone was using a hot plate to make porridge. Somehow the boiling gruel got knocked over and landed on my head. My mother became hysterical, and my father, enraged. She had never before seen him so upset. Apparently, my hair either fell out or was burned off, and it was so traumatic an event that I briefly stopped walking. In the photographs that follow this incident, I have very short hair and might be mistaken for a boy, my protruding ears on full display. To this day, I have a small bald spot where the hair never grew back.

Recently, I came across a New Year's greeting card from our DP-camp days. Written in Hebrew and wishing people a happy Jewish New Year, it features palm trees and, remarkably, a picture of my mother and me set inside the shape of a heart. We are propaganda, poster children for the Jewish National Fund, which sold these cards to DPs, urging them to explore a future in Palestine.

Alas, Palestine is not where my mother wanted to go. She'd had enough struggle, and she knew that DPs en route to Israel on illegal ships were often intercepted and sent to detention camps in Cyprus. Besides, she wanted to be with whatever family remained. Her first choice was Brazil, where one of her mother's sisters and two brothers lived. One of them—her uncle Solomon Weinberg—promised to help us emigrate. My father's closest cousins were in Israel, however, and I suspect that would have been his first choice, but he went along with my mother. There are so many what-ifs in my family narrative, among them how different our life would have been if we had ended up in Israel or Brazil.

I recently found, among my mother's stash of papers, a pile of letters from her Uncle Solomon and his wife, Chana, sent to my mother while she was in the DP camps, as well as one sent after she arrived in the United States. I think he was the first close relative to be in touch with us. I spent several days with my mother translating the letters as best we could. If my mother received other letters from relatives abroad, she didn't save them.

These letters, which span May 1946 to December 1949, are instructive of Uncle Solomon's intense desire to connect with family and to help, and also of how difficult it was for Jewish refugees to find a new home. Uncle Solomon had apparently sent money to my mother in Kolki, but that letter was returned. His relief in learning later that she had survived, remarried, and had a baby is palpable. They sent gifts to us at the camp, including a handmade silk embroidered dress for me, which I never wore because my mother said it was inappropriate for the DP camp. They did everything in their power to help us emigrate to Brazil. But it also became clear, as my family stagnated in Germany, that the barriers to entry had become increasingly difficult and, in the end, were impossible for us to surmount.

Also telling was Solomon's sense that what had happened to the Jews in Europe could happen again, elsewhere in the world. When my mother tried to connect Solomon and Chana with some Christian refugees who received permission to go to Brazil, he admonished her: "I didn't think you were so blind. . . . You know well that we lost six million of our best and dearest. The only reason they were killed was because they were Jewish. Your writing is so foolish when you tell me that Christians you met are going to Brazil and you sent regards with them. I don't want to see them, and, for you I have all of the paperwork guaranteeing that you will have work, that I am in good financial circumstances so the Brazilian government won't have to help you, and you are not able to get permission to come here." He added that Brazil let in only a few Jews, who, according to Solomon, pretended that they were Christian.

He went on at length about this, encouraging my mother to go to Israel: "All Jews who have the privilege to go to Israel shouldn't waste one minute."

His next letter came to us in the United States. He wrote that "I am very very happy you have finally found a place to end your wanderings," but added the warning that "there is also anti-Semitism in the beautiful good land of America." Uncle Solomon made another impassioned plea for Israel, apologizing for what he calls his Zionist passion. "If another Hitler will come they will try to do the same thing. If Israel is strong it won't happen again," he predicts.

And then, poignantly, "Write all of the time. I will answer. There are so few of us left. We must maintain our contact."

6

———

Just a few months before that last letter from Solomon arrived, in August 1949, my family boarded the USS *General Stuart Heintzelman*, a military transport ship filled with refugees traveling from Bremerhaven, Germany, to New York City. Toting my small leather suitcase, I was en route to my third country, a place rumored to have streets paved with gold. It would take time, but it would become our home. For my father, though, the distance of an ocean would not be enough to quell the suffering of his past.

I was too young to have many memories of our voyage, but I do know that my mother and I were both seasick for much of the Atlantic crossing, and we spent most of our time on deck taking in the fresh air, as did many of our fellow, equally green DPs. Apparently, I was dazzled by the bottles of soda in the vending machines, as well as by the oranges and bananas. Whether this was truly the first time I had seen fresh fruit or learned of these exotic carbonated beverages, I don't know, but clearly they made an impression.

Because the *Heintzelman* had originally been built as a World War II transport ship for the U.S. Navy, there were not

My parents, with me, as we leave for the US.

proper accommodations for families. Men slept in one part of the ship, women and children in another, which meant we didn't see much of my father, but at least we were reunited for meals.

Years later, when I tried to find a record of our journey, the only manifest that I could locate from the ship's August voyage was a list of crew members and "aliens employed on the vessel." Although the ships were built to transport 3,000 GIs, they now carried 700 to 800 refugees on these unique voyages. We were a special lot. From the manifest I counted 173 U.S. crew members, including cooks, waiters, butchers, and engineers. There was also a surgeon and four nurses, all of whom were clearly brought on board for this mission, because the manifest indicates they had been with the military for less than one month. Also on board were eleven "aliens" who were part of the International Refugee Organization, among them a Latvian doctor, dentist, three nurses, and escort officials, as well as Polish, Russian, and Ukrainian nurses, presumably the mix of nationalities intended to facilitate communication with passengers who did not speak English.

Since I couldn't find any listing of the passengers on board, I started to dig for information about the ship. I learned that on its first voyage in October 1945, the *Heintzelman* carried 3,000 troops to Yokohama, Japan. Less than a year later, in June 1946, the *Heintzelman* began the work of transporting refugees—its first trip was from Bremerhaven, loaded with 843 displaced persons en route to Australia. At that time, the United States had not yet opened its doors to Jewish refugees, but at least it provided transport to more hospitable countries such as Australia.

Finally, with the 1948 Displaced Persons Act, the United States cracked open its doors, albeit slightly and with strict immigration limitations. The initial DP Act said that 200,000 people could be admitted between 1948 and 1950. The act was then extended for two years, allowing approximately 400,000 displaced persons. It was blatantly anti-Semitic; only 80,000 of those admitted were Jews, while it has been said that as many as 10,000 former Nazis were able to come to the United States under this act.

President Truman told Congress that the act "in its present form discriminates unfairly against some displaced persons because of their religion, land of origin, or occupation. These provisions are contrary to all American ideals." But he nevertheless signed the act. To be eligible for U.S. admission under the act, a DP had to have been in Germany, Austria, or Italy by December 22, 1945. Most Jewish survivors from Poland and the Soviet Union had not yet had time to migrate that far west by the end of 1945. My parents were still in Poland in 1946, where I was born.

The act discriminated against Jews in other ways. For example, it stipulated that 30 percent of immigrants admitted to the United States had to be farmers. This was another subtle way of discriminating against Jews, most of whom were not allowed to own land.

The documents that I have from my mother and those available through the U.S. Holocaust Memorial Museum provide an incomplete and inconsistent story. Most of the important documents my family needed for entry into the United States under the DP Act were created and certified by officials in Ziegenhain in March, April, and May of 1949, just in time for our exit from Europe. My ever-resourceful father even managed to get himself certified by the International Refugee Organization in Kassel, Germany, as a farmer—and "a first-class worker" at that.

What is most likely is that my father knew people in Ziegenhain who could provide false papers both for me and for my parents, providing whatever dates were required. It is almost certainly the case that my parents decided that acknowledging my birth in Poland in March 1946 would have hurt our chances of immigration to the United States. What I have for a birth certificate is a document certified and stamped on May 4, 1949, by a registrar in Ziegenhain that says I was actually born September 8, 1946, in Ziegenhain. It makes sense that my birthplace was changed from Poland to

Germany, but why from March to September? I will probably never know the answer for sure. Though the logic isn't always clear, the result was.

We disembarked in New York City on August 14, 1949, and I stepped off the ship still carrying that suitcase, which now sits on a shelf in my dining room. Inside is a copy of my false birth certificate and an intricately knit blue sweater vest made by our dear friend Ruchel Brenner as a farewell gift. The vest is monogrammed with my initials, "ES," and it ties at the waist on each side with matching pom-poms. The tiny suitcase, now somewhat battered, also contains a business card for a curator at the U.S. Holocaust Memorial Museum, who wants to add it to their collection of artifacts used to tell the stories of the Holocaust and its aftermath. Eventually I will donate it, but I'm not quite ready; I am still using it to tell my story to my children and grandchildren.

Although my parents were not supposed to bring much with them, they arrived bearing gifts for the family that was taking us under their wing. Not just token gifts, mind you— they came bearing silver Kiddush cups and a silver menorah, as well as vanity sets with fancy mirrors and combs, and jewelry for my mother's two maternal aunts, Chia and Jean, and for her cousins. Clearly whatever my father had been up to both in Lodz and later, in the DP camp, had continued to be profitable. He carried a leather briefcase and brought with him a Leica camera, which back then was reportedly in high demand in the United States. In addition to the expensive gifts, my mother had a large diamond ring, probably hidden in a shoe or in the lining of a coat. Presumably my father also brought a fair amount of cash, because he seemed to have begun his life in America with more than the ten dollars refugees were given for their voyage and the five dollars handed out to each of us by the Hebrew Immigrant Aid Society (HIAS) when we arrived. However he managed to transport his wealth, he was lucky to have not been caught, since Allied occupation laws governing currency were strict. DPs were not allowed to possess foreign currency, and German currency could not be exchanged outside the country. Immigrants could use their German currency to purchase food to bring on the voyage but were only allowed whatever luggage they could carry along with the ten-dollar stipend.

Before we were able to leave Germany, we needed a sponsor who could guarantee us housing and would promise to employ my father so that we would not become public charges. My parents put an advertisement up at the camp, as well as in the *Forward,* the Yiddish-language daily newspaper in New York, in the hope of finding relatives. My mother provided her name, her maiden name, where she came from, and the names of both sets of her grandparents.

The name Bronstein caught the eye of someone in New York. It turned out to be the uncle of my mother's older half sister, Lifsha. Concerned that he might not want to sponsor her should he understand that she was not actually Lifsha but, rather, her half sister and not a blood relative, my mother wrote to him. His reply said, "It doesn't matter. Family is family."

My mother eventually connected directly with two of her Weinberg aunts in Washington, D.C. The story I have been told is that my childless great-aunt, Jean, whom I had always thought of as my "fancy" aunt, wanted to be the one to sponsor us. Unfortunately, that plan didn't work, because she had never bothered to become a U.S. citizen.

Ultimately, the husband of my mother's other aunt, Mime Chia (*mime* means "aunt" in Yiddish), became our official sponsor. Vigder Shereshevsky, also from Kolki, was not only Chia's husband—my mother's uncle by marriage—but he was also my mother's father's first cousin. If this seems confusing, all you need to know is that in Kolki, we were family in an infinite variety of ways.

The document, filled out on February 9, 1948, promised that Uncle Vigder, a U.S. citizen, would sponsor my mother, Etel (Etka), twenty-eight years old, and her family, including husband Leib Safran (Lejb), thirty-eight years old, and daughter Ester (me), two years old. Called "Individual Assurance by Relative," it further promised that, if admitted, my father would have employment as a watchman at the Barnaby Construction Company, "at not less than the prevailing rate of wages . . . and will not displace some other person from employment." Uncle Vigder had to further promise that "the principal applicant and the members of his family, who accompany him . . . shall not become public charges . . . and will have safe and sanitary housing at 5013 3rd St. NW, Washington, D.C., consisting of spare room in 9-room house occupied only by affiant & wife without displacing some other person from such housing."

We were met at the docks in New York by a representative from HIAS, who gave each of us our five dollars and a set of train tickets to Washington, D.C. Our HIAS document says the volunteer gave us each fifteen dollars, but my mother was certain it was only five each, for a total of fifteen. In matters like this, I trust her memory. My mother also remembered that the first person she saw when she got off the train in Washington was Uncle Vigder. He was wearing a white suit, and she thought he was a cab driver. He had brought an entourage with him—aunts, uncles, cousins, and a few relatives of our relatives—people we had never met and most of whom we didn't know existed.

What I doubt we realized is that we were walking into a terrible personal tragedy. This American family of ours had just lost the only child in their next generation—my almost-four-year-old cousin Mark, who would have been close to my age. My mother's first cousin Lottie, daughter of Chia and Vigder, had given birth to Mark Joseph Bennett on June 4, 1945, after several miscarriages and a difficult pregnancy. An otherwise-healthy child, Mark died after what was supposed to be a routine tonsillectomy just months before we arrived.

We spent our first days in America at Mime Chia and Uncle Vigder's attached row house on 3rd Street NW, the one described in our supporting documents. Who knows what they thought of having me around after just losing their only precious grandchild, but they nonetheless welcomed me into their home. I was a small Yiddish-speaking immigrant, oblivious to the fact that I was stepping into the vacuum created by the recent death of their grandson.

In my archives is a box marked "Shereshevsky," which contains all of Mark's pictures. I don't know if there is anyone else who has them. Years later, as I studied his photographs and tried to reconstruct these memories, I felt the sudden compulsion to visit the cemetery and see his grave. I have been to that same cemetery, Beth Shalom, in Capitol Heights, Maryland, many times before, for the burials of Mark's grandparents, his aunt and uncle, and his parents, Lottie and Abe Bennett, who rest on either side of their only child. His aunt, Bea Shereshevsky, was the last to pass away. Unbeknownst to me, she made me her guardian toward the end of her life. I was the one to make all of the arrangements for her care and eventually for her funeral—there was no one else. In all the times I was at the cemetery, I had never really looked at Mark's headstone, probably because I never knew him, even though I had been to the funerals of every other member of the family that surrounded him. When he died on May 7, 1949, he became the first in this line of seven to be buried in this plot. I am now the keeper of Mark's memory and that of his parents, grandparents, aunt and uncle.

Chia and Vigder's son, Izzy, used to say that my mother was saved from the Holocaust so that she could take care of her American family. She did, and then so did I. We had no ancestors left in Europe, and they had no descendants in America. All we had was one another. They came to my mother's family dinners and to my large, all-inclusive Passover seders, and we helped take care of Cousin Bea when she was struck with Alzheimer's.

Soft drinks and fresh fruit were just the beginning of many American wonders. Now there was this thing in a can called tuna fish. My mother remembered her first meal at her Mime Chia's house, which included tuna fish. She had no idea what it was. We had a lot to learn in America, and among the necessary skills was how to flush toilets—but not too often, since we needed to keep an eye on the water bill.

I also needed to learn English. But for the time being, Yiddish, my first language, seemed to suffice. Asked if I would like a gift, I requested a *shlafende lyalke*, a doll that opened and closed its eyes, something I did not see in the DP camp. I soon received several.

My parents were well taken care of during our first few

weeks in America, but there were few questions about what they had endured in Europe and how they survived. This was typical of survivors' post-Holocaust experiences in the United States and probably around the world. Survivors were urged to move on, and in so doing, they internalized the horror of their experiences. The general silence in my family about the past suggests that we were no exception.

In her 2007 book, *Case Closed,* Holocaust historian Beth B. Cohen examined the difficulties faced by the 140,000 survivors who ultimately made their way to the United States between 1946 and 1954. Using case records of Jewish social-service agencies, as well as interviews with survivors, she learned that immigrants were actually told not to dwell on the past. They were urged to find jobs and housing and to learn English. Actually, they weren't yet called survivors—they were greeners, or immigrants, or refugees, and they were regarded by some of their fellow Jews with embarrassment. Cohen notes that a Gallup poll in 1945 showed that 37 percent of Americans felt the number of European immigrants admitted to the United States ought to be fewer than that admitted before the war. Some members of Congress tried to cut quotas by 50 percent.

I suspect my parents didn't need this sort of advice from any social workers. They just got on with things as best they could. Fifteen months after our arrival, on November 9, 1950, my mother gave birth to my brother. He was named, in Hebrew, for our two grandfathers, Israel Srulach Bronstein and Yosef Safran. That was an easy decision, but my parents didn't know what to call him in English, so they entrusted an American relative, one born in the States, to come up with a name. The only requirement was that it be easy for my parents to pronounce, which is how Israel Yosef more than a little incongruously became Julian Edwin Safran.

I remember visiting my mother in the hospital for my brother's bris, eight days after his birth. Back then, new mothers were kept in the hospital for more than a week, and therefore the bris was in the hospital. This was the longest my mother and I had ever been separated. She wore a dark blue velvet robe, which she had brought from Europe, and to me she looked absolutely regal.

Oddly enough, given all of the pictures I have of our small family from Lodz and then later from the DP camp, there are very few documenting our early days in the United States. It's only now that I can look back and see that, the barbed wire in the background notwithstanding, the DP camp might have been one of the happier interludes in my parents' lives. They were young, surrounded by friends, and looking toward a brighter future. Once that future arrived, there was a whole new set of hardships—adjusting to a new life in a new country while trying to put their unspeakable losses behind them.

There are, of course, photographs from our time in America, but they are generally of a more formal vein: the occasional elementary school pictures of me, and a picture of my brother as a toddler. I also found what looks like a typical table shot at a bar mitzvah, probably taken shortly after we arrived. My parents both look young and handsome; I am seated between them, a little bewildered.

As far as I can tell, the first time the Leica was used in America was when I excavated it from my father's possessions and used it to photograph Frank after his birth, then, later,

Attending a bar mitzvah shortly after we arrived in the US.

Jonathan and Josh, and my nephews, Ben and Jeremy—all of my father's grandchildren.

The other photograph of my father in America is attached to a document of intention to file for U.S. citizenship, dated November 1949. He made it all this way but never became a citizen; my mother and I did, in October 1954, three months after he died.

At least the document gives me a good physical description of him: He was short, five feet five inches, and weighed 140 pounds, with hazel eyes and black-and-gray hair. One characteristic not mentioned is what we call "the Safran ears." My father had protruding ears. When I was little, after we came to America, my Aunt Jean thought I had protruding ears, too, and would Scotch-tape them back. Whenever my sons or one of my nephews was born, protruding ears was one of the first things we'd check for.

One reason that I know my father must have found a way to smuggle currency to the United States is that we evidently arrived with enough cash that one relative immediately asked to borrow half. My mother tells me that we got to this country with about $10,000, the equivalent of $106,036 in 2019. There was also money for my mother to shop. Cousin Bea took her to Mazor Masterpieces, one of the fancy furniture stores on 7th Street. Back then, this area on 7th Street, above Pennsylvania Avenue, was known as D.C.'s furniture row. Oddly enough, my thrifty, coupon-cutting mother had her heart set on a rather pricey bedroom set. She found one that she liked but wasn't sure whether to buy it. Seven hundred dollars was a steep price tag in 1949. Apparently, as she was hemming and hawing, Cousin Bea snapped at her. "Whose approval do you need?" she asked. "The president's?"

Why she spent so much I don't know. Perhaps she didn't realize there were cheaper places to buy furniture. Or maybe she just wanted to feel like a proper American, which to her involved a nice bedroom ensemble. Either way, she used this bedroom set for more than sixty years, so you might say it amortized well.

I'm not sure what I remember about my father and if what I remember is real. Although I have spent a lifetime trying to determine what happened to him during the war, the aftermath and the difficulties he faced in America are something I have actually tried to block out. Even now it is difficult for me to talk about him, and it has been hard to find the right words for this book.

There are many pleasant, colorful memories, of course.

Some real, some probably patched together from stories. I definitely remember going with him on his rounds to buy wholesale groceries for his store. He would take me with him to Union Market on Florida Avenue. This is now a chic D.C. shopping area, but back then the neighborhood was a mishmash of vendors selling everything from cigarettes and bubble gum with baseball cards to canned goods, fresh produce, and live chickens—all to independent grocers like my father. We'd hop into his jeep, or maybe it was some kind of station wagon, and go from vendor to vendor getting what we needed and also buying goods for another grocer, who had just emigrated and didn't have a car.

Sometimes my mother would come with us so she could pick up a live chicken for our own meal. We'd select the one we wanted and watch the kosher butcher slaughter it and pluck the feathers. At home my mother would have to finish plucking and cleaning the chicken.

Where the Italian grocer and scruffy kosher butcher once stood, there is now a gourmet food hall, with a bookstore and specialty retailers. Instead of live chickens, you can find gelato and olive oils from around the world.

I know little of my father's education or even of his life before the war, or what dreams he might have once had. One of his closest friends, Sol Aleskow, a fellow immigrant, told me many years later that my father was smart and that he hated the grocery business and wanted to do something else. One of his ideas, according to this friend, was to manufacture bumpers for automobiles, and the two of them went to New York to research opportunities. According to Sol, "He could have done anything."

Even if he wanted out of the business, my father kept

moving forward, selling, and then buying a new store. Now I marvel at how he was able to do this, to wheel and deal so successfully in a new country, in a new language, especially now that I understand what an incredibly heavy weight he carried. The home I remember best, and where we lived the longest, was at 1822 North Capitol Street. The store was downstairs, and upstairs were two apartments. We lived in one, and the other was rented to an older couple who lived there with their teenage grandson. At some point, they left and we moved into their apartment, just before we were supposed to relocate to our new store on 15th Street—the one in a better neighborhood and with more potential, or so my father thought. It turned out the owners of the promising 15th Street store had cooked the books and presented my father with false numbers. He had already given them $10,000, and he could not get it back. After my father's death, the owners would not give the money to my mother, either.

Driving down North Capitol Street after a meeting just a couple of years ago, I noticed that, like much else in this neighborhood, our old store was being converted to upscale condos. I parked and went in and asked the architect, who happened to be on-site, if I could walk through the building. The store was smaller than I remembered, but I was able to see where the butcher block had once been, where my father had stood, cutting meat for customers. The same butcher block where I once left my brown-and-white-spotted-dog piggy bank unattended for a few minutes. When I returned, the money was gone. My father was angrier than I had ever seen him. He yelled at me and said that I didn't understand how hard it was for him, by which I presumed he meant how hard it was to earn a living.

With hindsight, this was my father, under pressure, moving toward the end.

All these years later, I walked upstairs through the newly configured spaces and was able to find the place where my brother and I once slept, the room where we were on that Friday morning, July 30, 1954. I have a vivid memory of the light streaming in from the apartment window above as I sat on the floor next to my brother, who was then three and a half. We had a gray metal lunch box with a red lid. It was full of clay, and I was making petals, putting them together to form a rose.

My Mime Inda, my mother's father's sister, a nervous woman who'd spent much of the war in hiding with her husband and son in Paris, suddenly appeared. There was a lot of commotion. I have blocked out much of these events, but I believe someone may have told me that my father died. Perhaps they told me then. Perhaps they told me later. Another relative came to take my brother and me to a cousin's house. We didn't go to the funeral.

No one talked about my father or what had happened to him. Somehow I understood, even as a young child, that I wasn't supposed to ask. His death became part of the family canon of unspeakable stories that were to remain buried in the past. Years later, as an adult, I saw a death certificate, or some kind of official document, that clearly specified the cause of death: suicide. My brother independently went and got a copy, but he never discussed it with me. I'm not even sure how I know that, but I do. He told his wife, Sandy. And Sandy told their sons. And years later, one of his sons evidently told Jonathan—after he had already written a scene involving the suicide of a grandfather in his novel. But I never discussed it with anyone, not even my husband. When asked how my father died, I always said that it was war-related. I suppose it was, but not in the way that my answer implied.

I was about sixty years old the first time I spoke about my father's death explicitly. Reading Amos Oz's 2005 memoir, *A Tale of Love and Darkness,* in which he chronicles his own difficulty coming to terms with his mother's suicide, was a turning point for me. He had never spoken with his father about her death. Before reading this book, I had not even been able to use the word "suicide."

My father had a Jewish companion on the Nazi work detail that saved both of their lives, Srulach Zilberfarb. This is who he had been with when both of their families were murdered while they glazed windows at a distant train station. In November 2009, I met with Srulach's family in a café near my hotel in Tel Aviv. Srulach had already passed away, and, sadly, his son was dying of cancer, but his daughter-in-law, two grandsons, and one grandson's wife and baby came to the café. They brought pictures of Srulach, and although he lived a long life in Israel, he was described by his family as a man who was always haunted, who was bitter. "His eyes always looked down," they told me. "He could never really find joy in his new life in Israel. Even with his children it was difficult for him to express emotion and love." In the words of his daughter-in-law, "He never finished suffering."

Maybe my father felt the same way. He must have been haunted by the past, too. For all we know, he might have been suffering from a clinical anxiety and depression, something people in the 1950s didn't openly discuss. Perhaps his restless ambition had hit a wall with the purchase of the new store— the one he had come to understand would not be successful and into which he had already sunk a considerable part of our family's wealth. Perhaps this was the last straw.

Even with all of these factors in mind, I believe the Holocaust killed him in the end. Or maybe that's what I want to believe. There have been studies suggesting that suicide rates among Holocaust survivors were no higher than that in the general population, but there were nevertheless some notable suicides among them, including Primo Levi, Paul Celan, Bruno Bettelheim, and Jean Améry. Outlasting the war didn't necessarily mean you'd survived.

My mother chose to handle this tragedy by moving forward and not looking back, at least not in conversations with me. The three of us quickly moved out of the store where we had lived with my father and into a one-bedroom apartment in a building in southeast Washington, on South Capitol Street, that was owned by my mother's Aunt Jean and Uncle Bob. My mother became the resident manager, collecting rent, managing building operations, and taking out the trash at each tenant's apartment if the custodial help didn't show up. I tried to make myself useful. I was good with my hands and discovered a talent for fixing the venetian blinds, taking apart the broken slats, replacing and restringing them.

Quarters were tight: My mother and I shared the bedroom that accommodated her beloved mahogany bed and, beside it, a twin bed for me. My brother slept on the pullout sofa in the living room.

My mother and I used to sit on the lawn in front of our apartment and search for four-leaf clovers; I still have a sheet pasted full of the ones we found because my mother saved it. I'm sure it was a terrible time for my mother, but around her children she was always stoic. I don't think I ever saw her cry—not just then, but at any point in her life. It was only many years later that she told me she often thought during that time, "How come the sun shines for everyone else but not me?"

When I think back on how I dealt with this enormous tragedy in my life, I remember that I tried even harder to not cause trouble, to be a good girl and a diligent student. And to fit in. My classmates bestowed on me the superlative of having the most school spirit and elected me to give the class speech at lower school graduation. Subconsciously I must have known that I had to be the sun that shone for my mother. We protected each other. She didn't tell me about my father's suicide, and I didn't ask. This was our unstated pact.

A little over eight years after my father's death, my mother remarried. A cousin fixed her up with Rubin Kaplan, an easygoing man with a quick laugh. He was also a Holocaust survivor and, like my father, was in the grocery business. A recent widower, he had two young daughters: eleven-year-old Frances, and Judy, who was nine. I was sixteen at the time, my brother twelve.

We were two families of three, each missing a parent. Then, rather suddenly, we were a family of six. We packed up and moved to suburban Maryland, and my mother registered all of us in our new schools. There was no attempt to deal with the subtleties of blending our families, no conversations about the ways in which things might be touchy, or rough, especially considering that Frances and Judy had just watched their mother die of cancer. I'm sure there was love between my mother and Rubin, or love of a sort. But it was also a useful merger of two widowers, pooling their strengths and resources. Consider two Holocaust survivors, both widowed, working seven days a week in a small grocery store to raise four kids. The Brady Bunch we were not.

In many ways, this transition was probably easier for me than for the others. I was already well into my teens and relatively independent. I was active in a Jewish youth group, United Synagogue Youth, which meant that I had friends all over the country, including in our new neighborhood. I had one foot out the door, anyway—I was about to begin college, even though I'd be living at home while attending the nearby University of Maryland, and I'd spend summers working at the State Department and weekends on dates.

We all helped out at Kaplan's Market, at 17th and Florida Avenue, an area that saw its fair share of crime in those days. One Sunday I was working there with Mr. Gotkin, an older Jewish man who helped out on occasion. At closing time, we locked up as usual and headed out to the car. I had my driver's license by then and was going to give him a ride home. But as soon as we stepped outside, I was held up at gunpoint. The robber grabbed for the bag I was carrying, thinking it contained cash. I handed it over and he ran. Apples began falling out of a tear in the bottom of the bag. Mr. Gotkin and I quickly got in the car and locked the doors, the money safely in another bag.

This incident left me on guard—on the very rare occasions that my mother and Rubin went away alone, I kept a baseball bat by the front door, to protect the house and the other kids, just in case.

I'm sure there were happy times, but there were also constant low-grade anxieties—crime, finances, running a busi ness, and managing four kids—and most of the time, my mother and Rubin were exhausted. Still, they created a nice home, a place for all the family to gather on holidays, a place for out-of-town visitors to come for dinner, which was always home-cooked.

After college at the University of Maryland, I went to graduate school at Boston University, to study political science. My mother wanted me to be a teacher, to raise a family and take the summers off. I had other ideas. I held a series of political jobs, including a stint at *Congressional Quarterly*. That's where I was working when I was fixed up on a blind date with Bert Foer in 1970. He was in the army at the time, drafted out of law school during the Vietnam War. We married a year later, and together we moved to Chicago so that he could complete his studies at the University of Chicago. I found a job as the Illinois state press secretary for George McGovern's presidential campaign. It was a great opportunity and an exciting job; I even had the chance to go to the Democratic convention with the Illinois delegates. But I was in my mid-twenties, young and possibly in over my head. There was the time, for example, when I told reporters that the helicopter ferrying the Illinois campaign manager from Chicago to Springfield, where he was possibly going to file McGovern's election papers, had been stranded in a cornfield due to bad weather. This happened to be true and yet it was my first lesson in less is more, as journalists and political cartoonists looking for a little levity in their routine campaign coverage seized on the imagery of the helicopter mired in the cornfield instead of in Springfield, the state capital. It became the butt of jokes, including a cartoon in the *Chicago Tribune* and a mention on the national evening news.

After law school and the election, where my candidate was soundly defeated, we returned to Washington to be near both of our families. Our first son was born in 1974, then two more sons within the span of eight years. I worked a handful of different jobs in the public-relations and public-affairs arena, including running my own firm. We settled into a comfortable Washington neighborhood, joined a synagogue and became engaged in our children's schools, and while every aspect of it was remarkable to me as a wife and mother and a woman— each bris, each bar mitzvah, each soccer game and school performance and dinner-table conversation a wonder—it was also a relief to have it all be largely unremarkable.

Rubin, who had become a religious man in his later years, died on Christmas Day, December 25, 2003. They had been married for forty-one years. After his death my mother continued to live alone in the house for nine years.

She kept herself busy, going to exercise class and to synagogue and getting us to take her shopping. Because she didn't drive, and she knew that none of us had the time or the patience to stop at the six or seven different stores that would enable her to get the best deals, she strategically split the shopping among us, enlisting me, my brother, my stepsisters, and the grandchildren. I was probably the least tolerant and most frustrated of all. Eventually she realized that her friends in the neighborhood—many of whom were also Holocaust survivors—were dying and she no longer wanted to live there alone.

She decided to move into independent living in a nearby Jewish community complex in 2012. When she went in to discuss arrangements for an apartment there, she insisted on going without me or my brother. She knew we would just pay the going rate, and as always, she was determined to negotiate. A friend of mine, who was visiting his mother at the time, laughed and said, "There are no deals here." This was almost certainly true, but, regardless, my mother got a deal.

After three years there, she wanted out. She told me that she was afraid to stay in the apartment alone. In early 2015, I took her home for one weekend and that was it. Although we kept the apartment for several months, we could never convince her to go back, and she lived with us for the next three and a half years.

When it came time to move her permanently out of her apartment and into our house, my brother volunteered to take care of everything and said he'd arrange to get rid of the furniture and most of the clothes. She had never been big on material goods; she was not a collector of tchotchkes, like china or figurines. But she kept track of what was important and had detailed notebooks of her medical history and valued correspondence, all organized and neatly labeled, her photographs categorized in envelopes. I was grateful for my brother's help, but I sensed this was an opportunity to learn more, to possibly even discover more secrets, and I wanted to get into the apartment first, before it was dismantled. I wasn't after any possessions, and besides, she had already given away the few valuable things that she owned. She had given my stepsisters a gold watch and a gold necklace. She gave my sister-in-law the diamond ring that she brought with her from Europe. And she had given me a string of pearls, albeit with specific instructions to never have them restrung or to change the clasp. If they were refurbished, her thinking went, they would become just another string of pearls and not the ones from her.

In addition, she had always been very diligent about her finances, gifting money to her children and stepchildren, calculating what she needed to hang on to in order to complete her life. So it wasn't money or jewelry that I was after. It was something very specific: I wanted my father's suicide note. To be honest, I didn't even know for certain that one existed, but I suspected that it did. This was probably my last chance to find it.

Her sunny apartment was filled with furniture from the home she had shared with Rubin, including that expensive mahogany bedroom set she'd bought in 1949. She still had the same desk, and it was still stuffed with all of her old papers, including canceled checks, all carefully organized and labeled. Some dated back to 1949, when we first arrived in America. She had also clipped together copies of savings bonds that she'd long ago cashed. I looked through everything I could find, to no avail.

We kept working and packing and organizing her things, and after a few hours my mother and I sat down on her bed to rest.

"Where is it?" I asked, taking a leap of faith.

"Where is what?"

"Dad's note."

"I don't know. I don't remember," she replied.

I was pretty sure she was bluffing, so I pushed a little harder. "Okay," I told her, "let's just sit here until you remember."

She didn't move or say anything, and neither did I, for at least five long minutes.

Finally, she broke. "It's on the top shelf of the bedroom closet."

I walked to the closet and stepped onto a stool to reach the shelf, and sure enough, there it was. It was a sturdy box, 8½ by 10½, and 5 inches tall, and it contained much of what mattered to her most. It wasn't just an ordinary packing box but one that she had covered with Con-Tact paper that resembled a wood grain. I felt like I'd just unearthed treasure. Inside was a record of my mother's life: dozens of envelopes, each carefully labeled, containing letters and canceled checks. Some recorded the loans she had made. She had evidently been quite the financier, my mother, lending money and then recording the repayments and keeping the canceled checks. She also kept the letters thanking her for the interest-free loans. One was a heartfelt note from the wife of a grocer to whom my mother had lent money—she thanked her and pleaded with her to never reveal they had once had financial problems.

I suppose this wasn't surprising—that she would hang on to records like this. When she had moved out of her house and into the retirement community, she presented me with a shoebox, also covered with Con-Tact paper, containing letters sent to me by old boyfriends, organized chronologically and by the name of the sender. Obviously, she'd gone through them all.

I also found the canceled check for half of the down payment on the house she and Rubin bought. Other envelopes were organized by the names of her children, stepchildren, and grandchildren and contained the cards—even the Hallmark greeting cards—and the occasional personal notes they had sent to her over the years. One envelope was labeled *Ketubah,* in Hebrew, and sure enough there it was, the large decorative ketubah from my parents' wedding on Lag B'Omer in 1945 in Lodz, Poland.

There was also the largest and most elaborate Mother's Day card I've ever seen, dated 1950, and signed "Louis and Esther" in a fancy script that looked like it was written by a professional calligrapher. It had been our first Mother's Day in America.

And then, there it was, the envelope I was after, labeled, simply, "July 30, 1954." The date of my father's suicide.

There were actually four different notes, all written in Yiddish and in a mixture of Yiddish and English—Yidglish, we called it. On them was written the address, "1822 N. Capitol Street." Each note was numbered; the first two were written on pieces of the butcher paper he used to wrap meat in his grocery store. The last note was on paper torn from a small pocket spiral notebook, and he'd written different notes on the front and on the back.

"He said he loved me," was all that my mother told me about the notes on that day as we sat on her bed. She was strangely matter-of-fact in her delivery. But I can see now that this was what was most important to her—that he'd loved her. Or perhaps it was what she wanted me to know. Of course, she didn't need to tell me that; it was clear from the pictures taken in Lodz, and at their wedding, and during their time at the DP camp, that they were in love.

She couldn't know that what I longed to hear was that he'd loved me, too. When he killed himself, I was just a little bit older than the daughter he had lost, and my brother just a few years younger. When he looked at us, did he think of his first child? Were we too much to bear? These were not questions that I ever asked aloud.

I later had the suicide notes translated.

The first note begins: "My Etele is the best wife in the world. Forgive me for everything, my dear." He then asks my Aunt Jean and Uncle Bob to "take very good care of my dear little children and my dear Etele. Therefore, you will, God should help us, be rewarded."

The next note starts in much the same way: "My dear Etele and sweet little kinderlekh [children]. Etele, be good to our children just as if we were together. . . . They are diamonds. Etele, I wish for your happiness in your future. I end my suffering. The world is narish [absurd]. To my whole family I ask that you should please take good care of my little children . . . Also especially Etele. I ask everyone to forgive me for my terrible death."

The notes go on in the same vein. The final note says, "My sweet and dear little children. Be healthy and happy. . . . I am very sorry you have this misfortune. It must be this way. I am a mess of nerves and it is unbearable. My dear little children, you should listen to your mother." Signed, "Your father, Leibel."

7

On March 17, 1986, my sons surprised me with what they called a "coming-out party" to celebrate my fortieth birthday. We are big on celebrations in our family, commemorating occasions large and small, with everything handmade, hand drawn, home baked. The weeks of preparation are often more fun than the parties themselves. But no one was ever sure what to do on this particular date, the date of my actual birth. The boys—then twelve, nine, and three and a half years old—decided it was time to change that. They invited all of their friends and their friends' parents to our house, and they baked cupcakes and cookies with the help of one of our neighbors.

This was right about the same time that many Holocaust survivors and their families were reaching their own kind of tipping points. Anniversaries of pivotal moments from the war, like Kristallnacht, were at last being commemorated publicly. In 1980, Congress voted unanimously to form a council to create a memorial to the six million Jews and millions of other victims who died during the Holocaust, resulting in the U.S. Holocaust Memorial Museum. The first world gathering of Holocaust survivors took place in Israel in 1981, and Elie Wiesel won the Nobel Peace Prize in 1986. Popular culture took note, as well, when documentaries, TV miniseries, and major films on the Holocaust premiered: *The Diary of Anne Frank* was released as a TV movie in 1980; the film *Sophie's Choice* came out in 1982; and in 1985 came *Shoah*, a nine-hour-long French documentary about the Holocaust.

A new dynamic was taking shape between the generations as Holocaust survivors became grandparents, as was evident in our own family. While my mother continued to be reluctant to talk to me about the war, she was surprisingly forthcoming with her grandchildren, not only about what she had endured but also about the shtetl where she grew up. For me, these stories were profoundly tragic. For my children, who had more distance, they were stories of redemption and evidence of their grandmother's strength and superhero status.

This was a time of changing self-perception for me, as well. I was still trying to find my place and realizing that much of my narrative had been driven by a subtle rebellion. As a child I'd avoided hanging out with other "greeners," which was slang for new immigrants, for Holocaust survivors and families recently arrived from Europe, who tended to stick together, who were green and didn't know the American ways. And then later, consciously or not, I married someone who was not from that world. My husband, Bert, an even-tempered intellectual who has spent his career as a prominent, crusading antitrust lawyer, came from a family that had been in the United States for several generations. The Holocaust was something remote when he, a secular Jew, was growing up. He later told me that he learned about the Holocaust only years after it was over, when he went with his mother to the cinema and saw a newsreel from Europe that made her cry. It was a relief to become part of a family where people were relaxed enough to say what they thought, where jokes were told, where there weren't painful secrets. Bert's calm demeanor and encouragement, in many ways, enabled me to become who I am.

On a granular level, I also found myself rebelling against my mother's habits of deprivation. It was more than just the bargain hunting: She cooked everything economically, pinching on ingredients, saving grains of rice. On the occasion of the birth of one of her great-grandchildren, she presented a generous check—along with a bunch of coupons for Pampers. Even in fancy hotels and restaurants where we sometimes took her, she unabashedly slipped the rolls from breadbaskets on tables into plastic bags, which she then tucked into her pocketbook, much to my embarrassment. Who could blame her, this woman who once stole potatoes and hid them in pockets of her pants to survive? And in her later years, once she had moved into our house, I would sometimes find pieces of chocolate among the provisions she'd tucked into a compartment in the walker she used or hidden in her bedroom, just in case.

I, in turn, reacted to her behavior by adding a little too much extra everything. If there's a way to pay extra, I'm the sucker who probably will. I wanted to embrace life, not to scrape by, not to live in the shadows.

As certain as I was of my desire to live life to its fullest, even if that merely meant adding a little more butter or sugar to the recipe, I was at times uncertain of my role. I wanted to be the good girl—to not bring any trouble to this woman who had suffered so much. But I also wanted to find my own way. I wasn't trying to run from my past, and I knew I had a role in this story as the biological link between my mother, this strong-willed survivor in every sense of the word, and my children, three boys who came into this world with their own strong voices, with stories to tell. I was the hinge between these generations, but what did that mean?

It was not as though I had lost my way professionally—I had engaged in stimulating and exciting work in politics and public affairs for many years. It's just that what I was doing did not have much relationship to my central concerns or with these places back in Ukraine that haunted me. Then I was offered the opportunity to run Sixth & I in 2007, a new Jewish and cultural institution housed in a historic synagogue in the heart of downtown Washington, D.C. It was for me a dream opportunity to create and cultivate a new model for Jewish experiences and community that I couldn't resist, even though it was an unexpected shift into a new career, with a huge pay cut. And it came at a time when I might have decided to slow down a bit: I was already sixty years old and a grandmother.

All of the various threads of my life seemed to converge around this time. I was looking forward and I had the opportunity to circle back to where my family began: Two of the key people I was now in contact with professionally had roots in the same shtetl as my father. The family of Shelton Zuckerman, Sixth & I's founder and board chairman, was from Trochenbrod. In fact, we were distant cousins. It's a connection we had made years before, when Jonathan and Shelton's nephew, David, befriended each other in the same fourth-grade class. Bob Kogod, a major philanthropist and Sixth & I supporter who also happened to be a cousin, had family roots in Trochenbrod, as well. According to a map of prewar Trochenbrod, Bob's grandparents and mine lived literally across the street from each other—or, more accurately, across the dirt road.

It is only recently that I have begun to understand that finding these links is my calling, and it is only in the last few years, through archival research, through travel and detective work, that I have literally begun to connect the family chain.

With new resources available, both from my mother and from archives and databases and books, I began to seek out family far and wide, poring over old letters and documents, looking for far-flung connections when I traveled, and in later years, as the technology progressed, conducting DNA searches online. The unexpected discovery of one person would inevitably lead to another, with even more information, yet the more I learned, the less I realized I really knew.

While I was searching for family out of a genuine desire to understand and to connect, I had another goal, which in many ways fell into the realm of the fantastic: I hoped to find the family that hid my father, to actually speak to the man and the two women in that tattered picture, which at least represented something concrete that I could search for. I'm not sure that I really believed such a meeting would ever take place, but I wanted to try while there might still be time to find them. Of course, I had no idea where to begin; I couldn't even make out what was written on the back of the photograph, apart from what looked like the word "Augustine." And I didn't even know what Augustine meant: Was this a person or a place or just a random word jotted on the back of the nearest thing handy?

———

As a high school graduation present, my Great-Aunt Jean, the one I thought of as my "fancy" aunt, had taken me on a trip to Israel. With hindsight, I consider this the first step in my journey. She was my mother's aunt from a small village outside Kolki, and she became my de facto grandmother, as well as my bridge to what I thought of at the time as a more refined world. Jean was a formidable, aristocratic woman. People either loved her or did not; there was not much middle ground. She was a big woman—not heavy but large and well endowed, which was something that was hard to miss given her fondness for wearing revealing blouses, even late into life.

She had immigrated as a teenager, before the war, by sneaking onto a boat with a relative and, according to family lore, hiding under somebody's skirt. She made her way to Washington, D.C., and wound up creating what seemed to me a glamorous career as the giftware buyer for Kann's, a now-defunct department store on Pennsylvania Avenue. Accordingly, she knew and taught me about the finer things in life, taking me as a child to buy a pair of white gloves. She wanted me to appreciate quality, and even though she didn't have a lot of money herself, she had strong opinions on what one should and should not own. When Bert and I married, she insisted we have silver and china, for example, but she had to pick it out herself. "Honey," she told me, "you don't have good enough taste yet."

On one occasion, late in life, she went to New York and came back with a painting of a nude woman that we weren't quite sure what to make of. It hung over the bed she shared with her second husband, a sweet-tempered, considerate man named Harry Greenberg, whom she had known most of her life. Years later, when she moved into a nursing home and we cleaned out her apartment, we didn't know what to do with the nude; no one in our family was eager to claim it. I finally took it home and hung it, somewhat warily, in our living room. On one occasion when the rabbi paid us a visit, I was worried; what would he think of me, the mother of three sons, with this weird, risqué painting hanging on the wall? Who knows what he actually thought, but his only comment was to inquire as to whether it had been painted by someone famous. Truthfully, I had no idea.

Her choice in art notwithstanding, Jean opened up worlds to me. It was on the trip to Israel with her that I met, for the first time, close relatives of my father: three cousins who had known him growing up. They were amazed to meet me. They called it a miracle, and it was, in a way—with so few survivors, each family member you find is a miracle. I don't think I really knew what to ask, but, at least at the time, connecting with them was enough, and I managed to begin gathering tidbits of information about my father and about his mother's family, the Biskers.

Although I often wish I could have another shot at asking these now long-gone cousins more questions, this trip served as the catalyst for what would become my side career as the family connector, the hub of a network of people who sought out and then maintained contact with relatives far and wide.

Even though this generation was no longer around to mine for memories, in the early 2000s there was suddenly a new means of connecting with family—DNA testing. I had the opportunity to be a participant in genetically tracing ancestors when National Geographic asked to hold an event at Sixth & I for its DNA Genographic Project in 2008. To make their presentation more interesting, they proposed analyzing results for members of the staff, and, unsurprisingly, I stepped forward. I also volunteered a sample of my brother's spit for the test. The genographic work was aimed at analyzing historical DNA migration patterns rather than individual results, which came later in other testing. We didn't learn anything particularly interesting other than that, on the male side, our paternal line was heavily represented in the Mediterranean populations, most significantly in the Balkans and Greece and also in Sicily. Our paternal side descended from Africa, but our ancestors had apparently chosen to move north, through what is now Israel, then Turkey, then Greece. This possibly made sense: In Istanbul I had once seen a place called the Safran Bazaar—perhaps that market was owned by relatives. In Hebrew, *sefer* is the word for "book," and *sofer* means "scribe." And, of course, the name might be a derivative of saffron, the spice, which also has Middle Eastern roots.

Shortly after this experiment, commercial DNA testing exploded, with such companies as 23andMe making it simple to conduct research. It was fascinating, but it was also one more rabbit hole to go down late at night. I ordered kits for me, for my brother, and for Bert, and got the two of them to reluctantly participate. Over time I supplemented my research using tools like Ancestry, MyHeritage, and FamilyTreeDNA. Bert was pleased to learn that his results from 23andMe showed him to be slightly more Ashkenazi Jewish—97 percent—than my 94.7 percent. It was a meaningless difference, of course, but interesting all the same.

Bert also had significantly more close family matches than I did, which was not surprising given our different family histories. So many of the branches of my family tree were cut off during the Holocaust. Some of my matches were third or fourth cousins, with names I recognized. But an unfamiliar name—Cheryl Kahn—popped up as a second cousin, with a much more significant DNA overlap than any of the others. We connected and she told me that her grandfather, Max Bronstein, was killed in St. Louis in an auto accident in 1947, just before her father was born—or so she'd been told. I had a Great-Uncle Max who never married and died in 1994 of natural causes. We decided to have our parents do the DNA test. My mother tried twice and couldn't produce enough spit. Cheryl's father succeeded and tested as a first cousin once removed to both me and my brother, which is to say that my Great-Uncle Max was Cheryl's grandfather—the father of her father.

I was eager to embrace this new cousin, who is the same generation as my children. Cheryl and her husband, Steve, came from California to meet us. After the visit, I said to Jonathan that she really felt like family, and he pointed out this was because she really *is* family. And family she surely is— a recent study has found that basically all Ashkenazi Jews are thirtieth cousins, descended from the same 350 people some 600 to 800 years ago. But that doesn't diminish the bond we have: Cheryl calls me Aunt Esther, and I consider her a niece.

I became so good at navigating these sites and making connections that I helped track Bert's family, as well, and over the years I have forged networks that range from the Midwest to South America, from Poland to Australia. But on one occasion, I hit a wall. The DNA testing kits warn that you might discover relatives you didn't expect to find, which is to say that you might stir up a family scandal by discovering that some-one was the product of an affair. One night, I came across a first cousin once removed from Bert, named Kendra Moore. Bert and I were both puzzled—this was a name we didn't recognize, and the signs pointed toward something salacious. Bert asked me not to pursue this; he didn't want to know where Kendra, with this close DNA match, came from. I couldn't help myself, of course. I tried to contact Kendra Moore through 23andMe, but she didn't reply. Determined, I googled her, to no avail. After I had pretty much given up, she finally replied, explaining that she was actually Bert's first cousin once removed—Melissa Roudi, someone we knew well. She had gone on the website just out of curiosity and had used an alias. At the time, she'd been sitting next to a Kenmore air conditioner and decided to use the letters to make up a name: Kendra Moore.

One family scandal averted, I was able to keep my job as the Foer family historian. I even came up with the idea of having a Foer family reunion—something I had always wished for in my own family. Our own nuclear family, which now consists of three children and six grandchildren, is currently the largest branch of Bert's family tree.

Consider this family that likes to do it up big for every birthday, then multiply that by ten, and you will have a glimpse of what our seders are like. Our numbers may vary, especially as our family grows, but to give a rough sense of the size of our seders—I have hand-painted, from Ikea, a set of thirty-six Passover dishes. It's been a long project: I worked on the dinner plates one year, then soup plates the next, and finally dessert plates.

For me, Passover is not just a time to gather the family

for a meal and a rote reading of the Haggadah; it's an occasion to bring memory alive. We change up the narrative, we ask questions, we contemporize the story, we personalize it, we even turn it into theater. Storytelling is fundamental to resilience.

Each year we come up with a theme meant to refresh the Passover story. Some years we write plays and put out casting calls.

"Wanna be a star at this year's Passover?" reads the flyer from one year, which my sons sent out while they were still very young.

> To pick a character, just flip through your family's Haggadah! Some good suggestions are:
>
> > 1. Baby Moses
> > 2. Aaron
> > 3. Pharaoh (BOOOO!!!!)
> > 4. An Egyptian at the time of the ten plagues (He'd be pretty upset!)
> > 5. The pharaoh's daughter who found Moses in the water
> > 6. Moses's sister
>
> Come up with some ideas of your own.

Along with reviews from the previous year's seder ("Cowabunga!!! It was awesome, dude!!!!!") was the instruction to call Jonathan Foer, who issued the casting call, to avoid duplicating roles.

A somewhat more cerebral year, some fifteen years ago, we sent out questions for consideration that included:

- What is the relation between storytelling and history; between storytelling and memory; between storytelling and drama (reenactment)?
- How does the Exodus story transmit values?
- What is the difference between oral and written storytelling in Judaism?
- What special meaning can be read into the story this year, at a time when our country is at war in the Middle East, Israel's future is endangered, anti-Semitism is rampant in the world, American liberties are under siege at home?

More recently, our youngest grandson, Leo, has become a Civil War buff, so we found a way to integrate that into the seder—admittedly a bit of a historical stretch, but still a story about slavery. We even talked about how Jewish soldiers made seders during the war. Leo came dressed as a Union soldier, and we bought Union and Confederate hats for the other guests; Sasha, Jonathan's oldest son, was Abe Lincoln, complete with a Lincoln-like beard and top hat. Somehow we even managed to include all of the traditional Passover rituals.

Although it was at one time important to me to be able to seat everyone at the table, now that we have grown into such a large group we have moved the whole affair to the living room, where we sit on pillows scattered on the floor, as though we were having a seder in the desert. This enabled my mother to join us in her later years without having to get to the basement, the only place where we could fit everyone at one long table. It also allowed the younger grandchildren to move around instead of growing restless at the table.

My mother was always the star of our many seders, where she played a central role. One year we focused the seder on the story of her personal exodus from Europe to America.

My mother was actually Passover famous: She'd once taught Martha Stewart, on national television, how to make matzo balls. It was a segment meant to promote the 2012 version of the New American Haggadah, which Jonathan edited, and he had suggested that instead of talking about the book,

My mother teaching Martha Stewart how to make matzo balls on television with my son Jonathan, 2012.

he bring his grandmother along to give a cooking demonstration. In the green room, before the show began, she told the staff that she had survived Hitler, only to have them quip, "Well, then, you can survive Martha." And she did, to rousing audience applause.

———

Between the many Passovers, and in the margins of the car pools and the homework and the meals and the bills and all the rest of the minutiae of daily life that was both wondrous and mundane, I continued, on the side, to conduct my search. And although I managed to keep pulling the thread forward in incremental ways, there were no major breakthroughs until our middle son, Jonathan, took the project on himself.

As a rising senior at Princeton, Jonathan needed to come up with a topic for his thesis. He also hoped to spend the summer with a friend in Prague and was looking for a way to achieve both goals. I'm not sure how many ideas were floated, but I suggested going to Ukraine to see if he could find the family that hid his grandfather during the war. It was, of course, what I wanted to do, but I didn't have the courage back in 1998.

Jonathan was intrigued and I started working on logistics, putting together everything I could think of that might help with his mission. I made no less than forty copies of the picture of the family that hid my father, so that he could pass them out in Trochenbrod and in neighboring villages. I found maps of Ukraine in English and Ukrainian and marked the key shtetls he needed to visit, including Trochenbrod, where I thought my father was from, and nearby Kolki, my mother's home. In addition to supplying Jonathan with Ziploc bags, I sent him off with a dozen rolls of black-and-white film to document his journey. I felt that the photos he would take on this trip ought not to be in color, perhaps because that way they would mirror the few photos that I already had from this place, but also, without delving too deeply into my own psychology, black-and-white seemed more appropriately somber.

He was going to need a guide in Ukraine, so I put Jonathan in touch with Mark Talisman, the former vice chair of the U.S. Holocaust Memorial Museum, who was connected to a Jewish tour agency in Prague and could help him find a translator and a guide.

Although my mother knew that Jonathan was going to be in Prague for the summer, we didn't tell her about the other aspect of his trip. There was no way she'd be able to get her mind around the idea of her grandson going to Ukraine; to her it was the darkest place on earth, where the unspeakable had happened and, in her mind, could happen again.

That Bert and I encouraged this trip didn't mean we weren't worried, too. This was 1998, pre-cellphone days and before the world was wired for Internet, so for the five days he was in Ukraine—in this remote, often fraught corner of the world—we couldn't communicate with him. We called his roommate in Prague, Itamar Moses, to check in periodically, but he had not heard from Jonathan, either.

Jonathan began his travels by seeking out his grandmother's shtetl in Kolki, which was not difficult to find given that the town still exists and is on modern maps of Ukraine, albeit without any Jews. He wanted to go to the mass grave where members of our family were buried. At first, no one could remember where the grave was or how to get there—only that it was deep in the forest. Then finally someone remembered that a group had recently come through, inquiring about the mass grave, evidently hoping to dig up gold teeth.

Like something out of a dark fairy tale, there was an old woman who had shown them the way. Someone managed to find her, and Jonathan and his guide followed her into the forest, where they located the grave.

Before Jonathan left, the town's librarian gifted him a booklet on the history of Kolki, written in Ukrainian. She inscribed it with the message "Don't forget us." Months after Jonathan's safe return, by which time my mother knew of his trip, she read the booklet and observed that it never mentioned that the shtetl once had a sizable Jewish population. It was as if Jews had never been there at all.

Trochenbrod, or where Trochenbrod had once been, proved more difficult to find—a journey that Jonathan re-created in his novel to hilarious effect. After stopping everyone they could find along the way, he and his guide finally managed to arrive in what was Trochenbrod, only to discover there was quite literally nothing there. Even the roads leading to where the Trochenbroders once lived were gone.

Before Jonathan left, I had asked him to bring me back something for my memory jars—stones, dirt, anything. He said there was nothing there, not a wall, not a brick, not a nail, no indication whatsoever that this once-Jewish town had ever existed. When I asked him what he brought back, his message to me was: "There is nothing there to bring back; there is nothing for us."

In a sense, the fact that Jonathan couldn't find anything gave him permission to invent. He filled in this hole with fiction, and the fiction ultimately helped to produce fact. In this unexpected way, he not only put Trochenbrod back on the map, but he brought home a piece of my father to me.

Everything Is Illuminated, the fictionalized story about life in the shtetls of our ancestors, became an international best-seller and was published in more than thirty languages, awakening worldwide interest in Trochenbrod. Although nothing factual about the past was actually illuminated in his novel, it became the key to finding people who had information that would begin to unlock some of the deepest secrets of my family's past.

People with connections to Trochenbrod began to contact Jonathan and me—often to praise his book, and just as often to tell us what he got wrong. There were those who were outraged because they felt that the fictionalized account of Trochenbrod desecrated the memory of their town. Of course, many others were thrilled, including survivor Betty Gold, who now lived in Cleveland. She had written a memoir, *Beyond Trochenbrod: The Betty Gold Story,* and Jonathan's book gave her a platform to talk about her experiences in newspaper and TV interviews.

Then there was a call from a guy named Avrom Bendavid-Val, who left a message saying he knew the *real* story, and if I wanted to learn more, I should call him back. I didn't return the call for several years. I'm not sure why, apart from that I was inundated at the time. Family members have since suggested that maybe there was some other reason that I didn't reach out to him, some latent fear, perhaps, of what I might learn from someone in a position to really know, but, honestly, I think I was simply busy. I'd been receiving a huge number of calls in the wake of Jonathan's successful book, not all of them friendly, and I wasn't eager to engage with yet another person who was possibly calling to complain that my son's work of fiction took some liberties with fact. But when I finally did speak to Avrom, he became an important part of the journey.

Even after the initial wave of interest generated by Jonathan's book subsided, I continued to meet people who, sometimes very unexpectedly, added pieces to the puzzle. In 2004, at Jonathan's wedding to Nicole Krauss, Emily Kaiser, who was there as the date of Jonathan's childhood friend Stewart Ugelow, mentioned that her family came from Kolki; she wanted to introduce my mother to her grandfather, Philip Kaiser, who had been the former ambassador to Senegal, Hungary, and Austria. We arranged the meeting months later, which took place at the stately apartment of Phil and his wife, Hannah Greeley. We entered through a long gallery that led to a residence every bit as grand as one might imagine an ambassador's home would be. My mother was treated like royalty. There was a guest book open to a page that said, "Lunch in honor of Ethel Kaplan," and she was presented with flowers. The ambassador broke the formality by introducing himself as Pinchas Mayer, startling his oldest son, Robert, a journalist who served as managing editor of *The Washington Post*, who had never heard his father use his Yiddish first name. Over lunch at a large mahogany dining table, my mother held her own and didn't seem the least bit intimidated by any of this grandeur or by being in the presence of an ambassador. One thing she was eager to tell Phil was that his Kolki-born father, Moishe Bear, had been the one to offer to sponsor her immigration to the United States, when he saw a list of survivors that included the name Bronstein. She explained how she wrote back to him that she was not his niece Lifsha but actually her half sister and how he had replied, "It doesn't matter," that he would still sponsor her. My mother told Phil how she eventually connected with her aunts in Washington but that she never forgot Moishe Bear's offer and was glad that she could finally tell his son about it.

Robert filmed the luncheon, and Phil's niece Sarah Kaiser Hyams transcribed a recording of the meeting, as well as all of the interviews subsequently conducted over the course of a year by Robert's wife, Hannah Jopling, a PhD anthropologist. Sarah worked at the U.S. Holocaust Memorial Museum, opening up yet another new channel for information.

The lunch marked the beginning of a long friendship and a new branch of the family tree. My mother and I were even invited to a Kaiser family reunion. We were the only link to their cousin Lifsha. Until hearing the story from my mother, they hadn't known what happened to Lifsha and her two daughters. At the reunion, there was a blown-up photo of Lifsha playing a balalaika.

In 2007, after considerable diplomatic and political pressure, documents held by the International Tracing Service in Bad Arolsen, Germany, were finally made available to the public through the U.S. Holocaust Memorial Museum. This included information on millions of individuals, including my parents and me. When Sarah trained on the system, she used our names for the instruction exercise and found more than thirty documents. Sarah sent me scanned copies of the yellowed file cards that tracked our movements after the war. She also spent time going through the documents with me and helping me decipher them. Some were DP-camp records of our transfers from one camp to another, as well as health and work records and some general background information on my parents' movements during the war. The documents listed not two but now *three* different birthdays for me. Even though I didn't learn much new from these documents—that third birthday seemed an innocuous mistake rather than another deception—getting them was a gift.

The next wave of connections stemmed directly from babysitting duties. Our son Jonathan and his then-wife, Nicole, who is also a successful author, were asked to speak at international book festivals, and Bert and I were occasionally invited to come along and watch our grandson Sasha.

Our first stop was Brazil, where there is an annual book festival in Paraty—a beautiful small colonial town on the southeastern coast, with well-preserved buildings on its pedestrian-only streets. One of the attendees handed Jonathan a business card on which he had written a note: "My family comes from Kolki." His name was Marcos Chusyd and he lived in São Paulo. As usual, Jonathan passed the card on to me—by this point, he had moved on to his next book. I followed up, and after lots of back and forth we figured out that we were third cousins, from a branch of my mother's father's family that she didn't know survived.

From Paraty, we all went on to Rio. My mother had sent me off with contact information for Natan Kimelblat, who had come from Trochenbrod and had worked with my father in Lodz. "If you get a chance you should see him," she had said. Her suggestions usually paid off, and in this case, at least he was easy to find. This Trochenbroder had made it big-time as a prominent businessman: One of his jewelry stores happened to be right in the lobby of our hotel, the Copacabana Palace, an iconic Rio landmark.

With six-month-old Sasha in tow, Bert and I went into the

store, and I told the staff that I wanted to leave a note for Natan. Although I was always eager to forge ties with family, I didn't want to take away too much of our precious short time in Rio; I was mostly hoping to appease my mother by telling her that I'd tried. But the store manager seemed to sense the importance of our visit and asked us to wait while she called the main office. The next thing I knew, I was on the phone with Natan. He immediately understood who I was and said he was sending a car to pick us up. This wasn't part of the plan, so I told him I needed to check with our family about schedules and make arrangements for Sasha. Finally, I called back and said yes.

Later that afternoon, a car and driver pulled up to the Copacabana Palace, with Natan's brother, Itzhak, inside. In Yiddish, he started to tell me about my father and the business they had in Lodz. Although my own Yiddish was limited, I managed to piece together what he was saying.

As soon as we arrived in Natan's office, he looked at our wrists and scoffed, *"Schmatas!"* We were wearing cheap travel watches, and the next thing we knew we had quality Natan watches strapped to our wrists, perhaps the more appropriate timepieces with which to absorb the forthcoming revelations. These brothers had lived in Lozisht and had known my father and his family, including Choma, my father's half sister, who had gone to school with the brothers and married into the Kimelblat family. Both brothers had been part of a group of Trochenbrod partisans. They escaped the massacre in the village by hiding and then joined a Russian partisan unit in Belarus, where they carried out a number of heroic missions and were wounded. Later, they were recognized as war heroes.

After the war, the brothers went to Lodz, where they connected with my father and for about six months were partners in the so-called delicatessen that fronted what they confirmed to have been a money-changing business. These are the same men who posed in the pictures with my father in front of the business. Whenever someone questioned my father's right to own this business, he sent Itzhak, who now used a cane because of war injuries and had a chest full of war medals, to meet the general in charge of determining who had the right to which businesses now that most of the original owners were dead. My father figured sending a war hero was their best chance of hanging on to their establishment. Itzhak told me he asked my father what to say, and my father simply said, "You're a smart guy—you'll know what to say." Whatever he said must have worked; they kept the business and the currency flowing.

About halfway through the meeting, Natan invited his two daughters, Jane Rose and Miriam, who worked with him in the jewelry business, to come to his office to meet us. I recognized Jane Rose right away: She had been sitting directly in front of Bert and me a few days earlier at Jonathan's presentation in Paraty, and we had even talked to each other that day, without making the connection.

This was becoming quite the family reunion in Natan's office, and it turned out to be the first of many such visits. On a later trip, I visited Itzhak at his apartment in Copacabana, away from the beach. Frank has visited him separately there twice, as well. Each time we spoke to the brothers, we learned a little more. It was an important lesson. You need to listen, absorb, and then find an opportunity to go back and ask more questions.

Itzhak also sent me a copy of the book that he and Natan

wrote about their partisan war efforts, for which they were fêted and given medals by the Brazilian government. Originally self-published in Portuguese, an English-language version that he sent later includes a picture of Bert and me and our children; the Kimelblats describe us as their "American family."

On my next trip to Rio, Miriam Kimelblat took me to see her father for what would turn out to be the last time. Gazing out onto the sea from the balcony of his expansive oceanfront condo, which was filled with pictures of his children and grandchildren, he said touchingly, "You brought Trochenbrod back to me." He died the following year. A few years later, the business, one of the largest jewelry chains in Brazil, went into bankruptcy.

Back in the States, I finally connected with Avrom Bendavid-Val. He wasn't kidding when he suggested, in the message he had left me a few years earlier, that he knew the real story of Trochenbrod. Avrom, a Trochenbrod descendant, had visited for the first time in 1997 and then returned thirteen times and counting. Now he was enlisting me to help organize a reunion of Trochenbrod descendants, to be held in April 2008 in Washington, D.C. Settling on a location was easy enough: It had to be Sixth & I, the place that I ran, with its numerous unexpected ties to Trochenbrod.

There were close to 150 people from all over the country in attendance, including Sixth & I's board leaders and fellow Trochenbroders Shelton Zuckerman and Bob Kogod, my three sons, my mother, my brother, my nephews, Betty Gold from Cleveland, and Trochenbrod descendants from Seattle, Chicago, New York, and lots of places in between.

Avrom prepared a presentation of the vanished town we were there to remember. The final slide was of an empty field, faintly marked by a parallel set of trees and a tractor trail—all that was left after the Nazis killed all but a handful of Trochenbrod's approximately five thousand Jewish inhabitants (which at this point included Jews who had gone east to escape the Nazis) and the Soviets then razed the town.

"The first time, I have to admit, I didn't know quite what to make of it," Avrom said. "When I went there, I could see the traces of the main street, and I was very emotional because that's where my father came from. . . . I had to go back, and I had to find more."

By the end of the reunion, after tears and hugs, and with a few of the original Trochenbroders even connected to the gathering via telephone from senior-living facilities, there was talk of a group trip to Trochenbrod. Descendants who were now living in the United States and Israel would travel together to see for ourselves what was there and to bring memories of Trochenbrod back to life.

Someone created a video of the U.S. gathering to share with our fellow Trochenbroders in Israel, who had been well organized for years. They even had their own building, Bet TAL: *Bet* means "house of"; *TAL* stands for "Trochenbrod and Lozisht." They also had a website and regular gatherings, which were easy to organize given the country's relatively small size. The foundation for Bet TAL was laid by the early Trochenbrod Zionists—Trochenbrod had been a kind of Zionist hotbed, a place where parents were eager to send their children to Palestine—and then later supplemented by a group of partisans who survived the war. The key to the community's long-term viability was the genius of buying a piece of property in a place called Givatayim, which is close to Tel Aviv, and building a small synagogue so there would be a central place to gather. Income generated by renting out some of the extra space in the building is now used to fund gatherings and has even defrayed the cost of travel to Trochenbrod.

By coincidence, I was scheduled to go to Israel two weeks after the reunion, and Avrom asked if I would hand-deliver the video to an Israeli Trochenbroder. The trip was another babysitting assignment, this time to the Jerusalem International Writers Festival at Mishkenot Sha'ananim, where we all stayed and where the festival took place, overlooking the Old City of Jerusalem. The location was magical; with my grandson Sasha, now two, I explored the city parks, especially the fountains, which he could run through naked.

After we settled in, I called my Israeli Trochenbrod contacts, Chaim and Mira Binenbaum, to hand off the video. They offered to meet me where we were staying. They mentioned that they wanted to come to Jonathan's talk but had been unable to get tickets to his presentation. I assured them that if they came, I would find a way to get them in. They arrived early that afternoon so we would have time to talk first. Chaim is the Trochenbroder, and Mira, his wife, is passionate about Trochenbrod stories and volunteers at the Yad Vashem's research center. When they heard about my own interest, they offered to take me to meet some of the oldest Trochenbroders still alive, including a ninety-five-year-old former partisan who now lived in Haifa. Jonathan encouraged me to go, saying there was no point in waiting until my next trip to interview a ninety-five-year-old Trochenbroder. He gave me a day off from my babysitting duties.

Mira arranged the meeting for the next day, my last full day in Israel. She and Chaim picked me up in Jerusalem, about forty-five minutes away from their home in the Judean foothills, and then drove to Haifa for our meeting, which is normally about another two hours on the main highway. What none of us realized was that this wasn't going to be a normal day. It was May 15, and then-president George W. Bush was in town, causing traffic jams with ripple effects just about everywhere in this small country. We made it, eventually, using the Israeli mother of all navigation systems, Waze, to detour through back roads. It nevertheless took us several hours to get to the Haifa home of the spry Chaim Voitchin. It turned out he was not just any old Trochenbroder but one who had lived in Lozisht, which meant he might have known my family.

Before we set out that morning, I'd called my cousins who lived in Haifa, Sara and Rafi Bisker, to let them know I was on my way to their city. Sara and their oldest daughter, Gili, met us at Chaim's, where he welcomed all five of us warmly into his bright walk-up apartment. He described himself as a writer and occasional stand-up comedian.

I asked him questions about my father, Louis, or Leibel, Safran. I showed him the maps of Trochenbrod and Lozisht, pointing out our family's home. Even though it was near where he had lived, his face was blank. I tried again, showing him the map, pointing out where my grandmother had lived, one house away from her sister-in-law Sosel Bisker.

He stared at the map for a minute and then something clicked. "Ah," he said at last, "I was married to Raizel Bisker," and then added quietly, "but no one knows."

We all took a moment to absorb this startling information. Were we correctly understanding that this ninety-five-year-old man was nonchalantly disclosing the existence of a wife about whom no one—or presumably no one living—knew? It wasn't the first or last time that I heard about these other families, the secret families before the war that no one talks about, my own family included.

There was even more to come: I asked if he had known Choma, my father's half sister. "Ah, *dus is a mynse*," he said, which translates into, "Now, that's a story!"

He and Choma had apparently been close friends and confidants, and he knew that she'd been romantically involved with a man who was already engaged to a girl from another shtetl. Choma got pregnant, according to Chaim, and had an abortion. Her parents then arranged to marry her off to an *alter bokher*—an older guy. Chaim had the whole story. Choma's boyfriend married the other woman and eventually moved to the United States and had children.

This was fascinating, but it made no sense. If Chaim knew Choma, how did he not know my father? Again, finally, it clicked. "You mean Leibel the Lyscheter!" he said. "He used to come visit his mother all the time."

I had been asking the wrong question—or at least asking my question the wrong way. In Trochenbrod, no one used last names. They all had nicknames. My father wasn't known as Louis Safran or Leibel Safran. He was Leibel from Lysche. Leibel was his Yiddish name, and Lysche was the village that he lived in after Trochenbrod. I'd also failed to account for the fact that family life could be messy. My grandmother, by this point, was no longer Brucha Safran: She had remarried and changed her name to Kuperschmit. This meant that my father's half sister was Choma Kuperschmit. No wonder it took a while for Chaim to understand what I was after.

It had been a remarkable meeting. Before we left, Chaim asked for a kiss from me and my young cousin Gili. Gili and I gave him a peck on each cheek at the same time.

After the meeting, we went back to my cousins' ultra-modern apartment on the top of Mount Carmel, overlooking Haifa Bay. Mira, absorbing all of this new information, started working the phones, calling other Trochenbroders. After some initial warm-up chitchat, she would ask whether they had known my father, Leibel from Lysche. The first few calls didn't produce anything. Finally there was Nachman Roitenberg, who told Mira, "If I don't know him, no one does," the implication being that he knew everyone in the shtetl—but then, after a beat, he said, "You know, I think that Fanya Rosenblatt might know him." Perhaps Nachman didn't know my father, but I realized later that in a 1947 photograph of Trochenbrod survivors, he is standing right next to him.

It was now about 8:00 P.M. We were driving back to Jerusalem from Haifa when Mira asked if she should try to reach Fanya.

"Absolutely," I said, despite the fact that it was getting late and I had to be at the airport at 5:00 A.M.

"Of course!" Fanya said, when Mira reached her by cell-phone. "Of course I knew Leibel from Lysche!"

And so we detoured, this time to Bnei Brak, a center of ultraorthodoxy on the central Mediterranean coastal plain, just east of Tel Aviv. Strangely, I knew of this place because the name appears in the Haggadah, in the Passover seder. It is where Rabbi Eliezer, Rabbi Yehoshua, Rabbi Elazar ben Azariah, Rabbi Akiva, and Rabbi Tarfon discussed the Exodus all night, until their students arrived to tell them it was morning and said to them, "Rabbis, the time for reciting the morning Shema has arrived." And now here I was, going to Bnei Brak at night to unearth whatever memory might be possible about my own family's exodus.

Unbelievably, hours later, Bush's visit was still creating travel headaches. Again, Chaim used Waze and we crisscrossed our way along back roads. We drove for at least another hour before arriving at Fanya's house, a little after 9:00 P.M.

We were barely inside the door when she pulled me aside and asked, "How did this tragedy happen?" She was referring, of course, to my father. How she knew about his suicide, I'm not sure. We fell into each other's arms in her tiny hallway and both cried, out of sight of Mira and Chaim. She asked me to come back and spend a few days with her in her house. How I wish I had. The next time I visited her, she was descending into Alzheimer's.

I remember being impressed by her; my notes describe her as a "classy lady." She had a lovely garden out front; inside, the house was neat, and her dining room was lined with walls of books. Included in her impressive collection was a book written by Fanya's husband, Gad Rosenblatt, who, along with our new acquaintance Chaim Voitchin in Haifa, had been one of the Trochenbrod partisan heroes. They had served in the same unit as Itzhak and Natan Kimelblat, and all had survived. Gad had just died six months earlier.

Fanya was the first person I met who had known my father before the war, apart from his cousins. Like him, she had ties to Trochenbrod but had lived in a small village nearby, called Chetvertnia, which was right next to Lysche, where my father and his family lived. In contrast to all-Jewish Trochenbrod, there had been only a handful of Jews in these villages.

I hung on her every word. She described my father as a

"*chevra* man," a person who could make friends, or do business, with anyone. She pointed to her coffee table and said, "If Leibel were here, he could even make friends with the table."

This was definitely consistent with the father I had known—friendly and charming, despite the darkness inside. I loved hearing this, but it also made me ache. I wanted more. I wanted to excavate every detail from her that I could.

"Can you tell me anything more about him?" I pleaded.

"He could do anything with his hands," she said, which was unsurprising. I knew this from my childhood, and it also made me think of our youngest son, Josh, who had inherited this trait.

Hesitantly, I finally asked her the question I'd been carrying around with me since that day in my mother's pink kitchen. Did she know anything about my father's first wife and child?

"Tzipora," she said. "That was the name of his wife."

Did she know about the daughter? I was on the edge of my seat, on the verge of learning the name of my sister, at last. But it was not to be. She knew Leibel and Tzipora, she said, but she couldn't remember anything about their child.

The details of mass murder of the Jews in Chetvertnia has been well documented by Yahad-In Unum, an organization founded in 2004 and led by Father Patrick Desbois, a French Catholic priest who has devoted his life to chronicling these massacres, collecting evidence and interviewing eyewitnesses.

Yahad estimates that between 1.5 and 2.2 million Jews were murdered in the Holocaust by bullets. No one knows the exact number, and we probably never will, because there were few survivors. These numbers are based on witness interviews and forensics done at each of the mass graves. Yahad-In Unum, which means "together" and "in one" in Hebrew and in Latin, is dedicated to locating and thoroughly documenting the mass graves of Jewish victims of the Nazi mobile killing units—the *Einsatzgruppen*—in the former Soviet republics. Father Desbois's work has been sanctioned by the pope, recognized and encouraged by the president of France, and supported in Europe and the United States.

Witnesses told the Yahad team that there were about 120 Jews in the ghetto in Chetvertnia, including those from Chetvertnia, Lysche, and several other rural villages. The Germans had arrived in the village at the end of June or early July 1941 and forced the Jews to wear yellow badges, presumably Jewish stars. In December 1941, all of the Jews of Chetvertnia and those rounded up from the neighboring villages were confined to a ghetto that was behind barbed wire and were forced to do hard physical work.

The ghetto was liquidated on October 10, 1942, two months after the Jews were murdered in Trochenbrod and Kolki. Fanya said they knew about what had happened in Trochenbrod, but they somehow thought, or at least hoped, they would be spared because they were doing forced labor, which was mostly farm work, and were in an out-of-the-way rural ghetto.

How did my father and Fanya escape being murdered? I asked. Although I knew the answer, or at least the partial answer, I found that by asking the same question of different people, I was often able to collect new details.

Fanya said there were only three survivors from the ghetto: my father, Srulach Zilberfarb, and Fanya. I had heard bits of the story and knew my father was with someone else, but at that time I'd never heard Srulach Zilberfarb's name. As I knew, my father and Srulach had been on a Nazi work detail when the Jews were brought to a pit and shot. Now Fanya told me that the morning of the mass murder, her mother saw soldiers stationed outside and sensed that something bad was about to happen. She convinced Fanya to hide inside the sofa, by which she presumably meant that she buried herself under the cushions. She survived; the rest of her family, her parents and siblings, were murdered, as were my father's wife and child and Srulach Zilberfarb's family.

A witness to the murders told the Yahad team that he had been nearby, with his grazing cows, when the Jews appeared in a line, their hands tied with rope. One German brought them to the pit, he said, and then made them undress completely before climbing down into the open grave, where another German shot them.

A couple of meters from the pit was a table and chairs, and the Germans would take breaks, fortifying themselves with food and liquor for the next round of executions. Local police participated, as well. Another witness reported that, after they finished, the grave moved for days. There were some who survived, for a time, beneath the earth.

Fanya, Leibel, and Srulach found one another a few days later and met in the dark on a bridge in Chetvertnia, late at night. Leibel told her that he and Srulach were hidden together briefly by a family that Fanya described as "not typically Ukrainian." She wasn't sure what happened to my father or Srulach after that. Fanya hid in the forest until a Ukrainian she knew found her a job as a housemaid. She took a false identity and worked for a German who did not know she was Jewish.

This was the first time I had met someone who had been with my father during the war. I was overwhelmed and exhausted, and it took me a while to process what she told me. Honestly, all these years later, I'm still trying to make sense of it.

While we were sitting in her living room, Fanya tried to find contact information for the family of Srulach Zilberfarb, with whom she was very close. His son and daughter-in-law lived in Israel, she said, along with their sons. I met them on the next trip.

Armed with all of these important new clues, I knew that at last I had to go to Ukraine.

But, first, I had a bit more digging to do.

8

More than seventy years after Trochenbrod's destruction, its story was still being told. New bits of information continued to emerge. The fictionalized shtetl was brought to the screen in 2005 in a motion picture based on Jonathan's book. Three years later, my friend Avrom, along with filmmaker Jeremy Goldscheider—another Trochenbrod descendant—decided to tell the real story of the shtetl in a documentary.

Avrom and Jeremy were looking for sponsors to help fund their project. I stepped forward with a contribution and a request. I sent Avrom a copy of the picture of the family that we thought hid my father and told him the name of the village, Lysche, that I had learned from Chaim and Fanya on my recent trip to Israel. Lysche was close to Trochenbrod—or what had once been Trochenbrod—where their crew was going to be filming. I asked whether they would be willing to show the picture to local residents, to see if they could find someone who might be able to make sense of it.

Avrom, along with his young translators, Anna Kurnyeva and Sergiy Omelchuk, and Jeremy and his film crew went to

Lysche, a village that is now called Krynychne. As soon as they reached the village, they began to show the picture to the various small groups that gathered to see what was going on; a film crew descending on this remote village was hardly the norm, and they attracted a fair amount of attention.

It didn't take long to make a connection: An old woman with a scarf wrapped around her head took a look at the picture and recognized my father right away, telling the crowd, "That's Davyd and Leibel." She knew my father's name as well as the name of the other man and the man's daughter, Katarina. She wasn't sure who the second woman was, but she had no doubt about the others. Then, remarkably, she told the Americans and their translator that Davyd's grandson, whose name was Mycola, still lived in the family home, just down the road.

Avrom, Jeremy, and their entourage headed straight to the house. Mycola, whose last name they learned was Lishcuk, and whose grandfather was Davyd Zhuvniruck, lived by himself. Although they didn't learn much from their conversation with Mycola, they had the opportunity to look around the house and to zero in on the many photographs on display in the main room. They compared my picture to the ones on the wall and took photographs of my photo beside them. They were all convinced that this was for real, that these were the same people.

I started corresponding with Avrom's translator Anna and asked her to make contact with Mycola's sister, Nadiya, who was now the family matriarch, and his brother, Victor, a physics teacher. I had so many questions that I didn't know where to begin. Were there more pictures? Did they have a match to the picture that I had? Who had lived in the house during the war? What did they know about my father and his family? Was there anyone still alive who had lived in the house during the war and who knew what happened?

I learned that Nadiya's mother, Katarina, who was in my picture, had died. Nadiya agreed to look for other photos that might exist from that time, but she wasn't hopeful; unfortunately, she explained, she had a specific childhood memory of her mother putting a bunch of old photographs inside the drawer of a table and then setting the table on fire. This was astonishing; photos were a luxury back then, and there were very few of them. Why would she want to destroy them? I had a theory. I remembered a detail from the story my mother had told me about the man who had helped hide my father, that he had suggested, after the war, that my father return to the village to marry his daughter. Perhaps burning the photos, if this story was true, was the result of the perceived rejection.

Shortly after Avrom returned, he came over to my house to discuss the trip. Both he and Anna were convinced they had located the descendants, and he wanted to personally present the findings. We looked at the photos on a big television screen. The resemblance was certainly impressive, but I nevertheless remained skeptical. As Anna put it, they were 90 percent certain, but that last 10 percent was up to me.

Meanwhile, I was hearing details about the forthcoming Bet TAL trip to Ukraine. I knew that I had to get on the plane and confirm that final 10 percent myself.

Once the trip became a reality, Bert and I started to look at logistics. He understood, perhaps better than me, that I would need emotional support. He offered to accompany me, but he felt the trip would be more meaningful if I shared it with one of our sons—it was, of course, their story, as well.

I learned years later that all three of my boys were concerned about how I would handle the trip, fearful that I might be slammed by some sort of emotional tsunami. Frank volunteered right away, and he was the perfect companion. As a journalist, he knew the trip would be interesting, but on a personal level, although he might not have realized it then, he was also searching—for his family's history and for the grandfather he had never known.

Frank was, at the time, the editor of *The New Republic*, and he had recently written the book *How Soccer Explains the World*. Naturally, he was going to do his own research before embarking. He began contacting scholars at the U.S. Holocaust Memorial Museum. He also reached out to Timothy Snyder, a prominent historian and author who teaches at Yale, to get more information on the obscure villages of Lysche, where my father and his family had lived, and Chetvertnia, the ghetto where my half sibling was murdered.

I began to do my own reporting, as well, some of it formal, some of it impromptu—such as the time our friends Jonathan Cuneo and his wife, Mara Liasson, a political reporter for National Public Radio, were visiting. We spoke as their son played on our floor, digging into our stash of toys. Jon is an antitrust lawyer who had worked with Bert, and he'd recently been the lead counsel on a case involving what was known as "the Hungarian Gold Train." This concerned a train that had been stopped in Austria by Americans in 1945. It was en route to Berlin, and turned out to contain stolen Jewish property ranging from paintings and jewelry to rugs and various valuable personal items—virtually none of which was returned to the families. Jon had won restitution for the Holocaust survivors from the U.S. government. Because of his recent involvement in the subject, he was intrigued by my family history, and he told me stories about his own parents, who had both worked in intelligence activity during World War II—his mother for the British and his father for the United States.

I showed Jon the photographs I had received from Anna in Ukraine to get his opinion on whether he thought there was a match. He suggested I get a professional investigator to take a look and recommended contacting the Academy Group, which was made up of former FBI agents, people with whom he had worked. What a great idea, I thought. Why mess around with my own amateur sleuthing when I could go to the FBI?

I put in a call the next morning. The receptionist transferred me to Peter Smerick, who had spent more than twenty-five years at the agency as one of the FBI's four experts in forensic photography and criminal profiling. After I explained my story, former agent Smerick informed me that he charged $250 an hour and I would probably be wasting my money because it was unlikely that he could tell me anything definitive based on what little I had. I was undeterred. If I was about to go all the way to Ukraine, I could take my chances on a trip to Manassas, Virginia, to see what I could learn from a former FBI forensic-photography expert. I felt the money would be well spent.

On Friday, June 26, about six weeks before my trip, I took the day off from work and drove about an hour to the Academy Group. Peter showed me around his office, which was furnished with framed awards and newspaper clippings of major investigations he had handled. He had profiled David Koresh, leader of the Branch Davidians in Waco, Texas, and had testified before Congress about that. He had been involved in the case that inspired the movie *The Silence of the Lambs*. He seemed particularly proud of "the Freckle Case," in which he identified a murderer who had been on the loose for eighteen years by mapping the moles and freckles on the perpetrator's hands. Smerick told me he was of Ukrainian descent, so he was sympathetic to my mission of finding this Ukrainian hero who had saved a Jew during the war. We spent an hour together, comparing the pictures Anna had copied from the house in Krynychne, and the picture that my mother had given me.

We used a crosshair magnifier and a measuring stick to compare distances between facial features. We measured distances between eyes, ears, lips, noses, and earlobes, which Smerick said can be unique identifiers. After close examination, he identified specific features of the rescuer in my picture: He had short eyebrows, elongated ears, and unusual eyeballs.

So, what did we have? He said that he couldn't honestly conclude that the people in both pictures were the same. I was disappointed, hoping for a positive confirmation so I could resolve my mystery. There was a dramatic pause, and then the former FBI agent added that he also couldn't say that they *weren't* the same people.

Knowing I was soon going to Ukraine, he gave me advice on what to look for when I got there. I should try to look at originals of the photos and hopefully compare more pictures that the family had. He urged me to try to do some of the same measurement exercises we had performed in his office on the original photos, and he showed me how to do this without his equipment. I should try to assess the angle at which the picture was taken, for example, because that impacts facial features. He told me to ask where and why various photos were taken. And, most important, he said, if I couldn't get a perfect identification of the faces, would be to look at the clothing people wore in the photographs. My picture had been taken in Ukraine, presumably in the early 1940s, a time and place when people didn't have large wardrobes. People likely had a set of special clothes that they wore for important occasions, including having family photos taken, he said, so this would be another thing to compare.

Frank asked his colleague Leon Wieseltier, an author who was, at the time, literary editor of *The New Republic,* to meet with us before the trip. Leon, also the child of Holocaust survivors, had recently been on his own Ukraine trip. He tried to manage our expectations, telling us that all he'd hoped for, and ultimately all he really got, was the opportunity to walk the roads and breathe the air of his ancestral shtetls. In the end, he said, that was enough. But he did mention a detail that stuck with me: He had brought with him a copy of his book *Kaddish* and left it behind, explaining to his befuddled guide that he wanted to leave a piece of himself in this place where his family had come from.

During a dinner at around the same time, I wound up in conversation with an old friend, Sandy Berger, President Clinton's former national security adviser. I told him I was going to the Ukraine and he startled me by saying, "No, you're not."

He went on to explain that I was going to *Ukraine,* not to *the* Ukraine. The country had been at one time the Ukrainian

Republic of the Soviet Union, which, translated, means Bor-
derlands. The country did not want to be referred to as the
borderland. This was useful advice. I suppose you might say
that I had the national security adviser involved, as well as
the FBI.

I had collected a lot of useful background material as well as
good advice, but I wasn't quite ready yet. In addition to the
photographs, I needed good maps. I remembered that on our
visit to Ambassador Phil Kaiser's apartment in 2005, I had
spotted a framed old map of Kolki in the hallway. It was so
detailed that you could literally see every house, as well as the
river and the handful of streets, and it brought the place alive
for me. Phil told me that his sister-in-law had copied it from a
map she'd seen at the Library of Congress. Now I asked to
borrow it so that I could make my own copy.

When Jonathan had gone off to Ukraine in 1998, I went
to a map store, an establishment that has since been driven
out of business by the Internet and the advent of navigation
systems. I had purchased a few maps and circled the two
shtetls he was going to visit, Kolki and Trochenbrod.

Now, roughly a decade later, the map store was gone, and
so instead I was off to the Map Room of the Library of Congress in the Madison Building, armed not only with the various names of the shtetls I had known about in 1998 but also
with new, key information about additional shtetls I had identified in my research.

As with everything about this subject, the more I learned,
the more complicated the story became. When Jonathan took
his trip, we had all been surprised that he was going to Ukraine

rather than to Poland, which is where my mother had reported her family lived. That said, she never thought of herself as a Pole. It had been confusing at the time, but now I understood why. This is a part of the world that changed hands eight times between 1914 and 1945: It was part of the Austro-Hungarian Empire, then Russia, Austria, western Ukraine, Poland, the Soviet Union, Germany, the Soviet Union again—and now it was Ukraine. My parents' neighbors had been Ukrainians, Poles, and Jews, mixed with the various occupiers, including Russians and Germans. The shtetl names had changed, too, depending on the occupier. I needed all of this information as I searched for maps. My father had grown up in Trochenbrod, but the shtetl had also been called Zofjówka in Polish, Sofiyevka in Russian, and Trokhymbrid in Ukrainian. For my mother's town, the name changed only slightly from occupier to occupier and resident to resident. Her town is Kolki in both Russian and Polish, and in Yiddish and German it's Kolk.

Even without these challenges, one could spend a lifetime burrowing in the Geography and Map Division of the Library of Congress; there are more than 5,000,000 maps, 80,000 atlases, and thousands of other items including globes and plastic relief materials. I spent hours doing computer searches and going through the old-fashioned file card catalogs and was able to find and print dozens of maps of the region from the various occupiers, including Poland, Austria-Hungary, and even Germany, with all of them marked in the appropriate languages.

In order to ensure I had the right places, I plugged in the longitudinal and latitudinal coordinates. It was fascinating to be able to track the growth of the shtetls over the years and to see the changes made by the various occupiers at the same time that the geography remained largely the same. I loved studying the maps and copied as many as possible during the hours that I was there.

The two most important maps that I found didn't come from the Library of Congress or the Internet but had been handmade by people who lived in these shtetls. One was created by survivors of Trochenbrod. Sometime after their arrival in Israel and before their memories began to deteriorate, Trochenbrod survivors gathered in a room of their beloved Bet TAL, in Givatayim, in suburban Tel Aviv. They sat in the room arguing about who had lived where on the long straight road through Trochenbrod that veered off to form Lozisht. After a day of heated arguments, they finally agreed on a map showing where they and all of their neighbors lived, which was ultimately printed, with each resident's name in both Hebrew and English.

The second map is one that I drew with my mother to try to figure out where our family had lived and to record the names of the neighbors and the location of the river and the market, in hopes that it would help me navigate Kolki when I arrived. My mother had never learned to drive and didn't have the best sense of direction, so I wasn't sure how helpful our hand-drawn map would be, but it was still infused with the sort of detail that no one else could provide.

A month before leaving for Ukraine, Bert and I were in Paris, and I made an appointment with Father Patrick Desbois, the founder and head of Yahad-In Unum, whose headquarters were in the city.

Yahad-In Unum's offices were, at the time of my visit, in

an unmarked building on a major street in Paris. They have since moved just outside Paris, for security reasons.

Bert and I sat with Father Desbois for about an hour, talking mostly about how to plan my upcoming trip to Ukraine. His advice was priceless: He told me to be relaxed and to keep my questions simple, to ask people to focus on stories about life in the village and about their families. Otherwise, he warned, they might be on guard, worried that I had some other objective, like reclaiming family property that had been lost during the war. He also suggested that we return and interview people a second time, that in his experience people often remembered new things the next day. And he warned me, ominously, that Lutsk, the city where my parents had met and where my hotel was located, was the most anti-Semitic part of the country—"two hundred percent anti-Semitic," in his colorful words. He offered to put me in touch with his translator and his bodyguard, which I considered, but it turned out that his contacts there spoke better French than English. Besides, I already had Anna Kurnyeva lined up, and she was invested in my story and had even arranged for her father to be our driver. Ultimately, I decided against hiring a bodyguard. Father Desbois was well known for his work, and he was a controversial figure in Ukraine. I figured that no one would know, or particularly care, who I was.

There was one other important bit of preparation before buying airline tickets and embarking on this trip: I had to find a way to tell my mother. Ukraine was where all of her family was killed by the Nazis, while neighbors watched and sometimes helped. She had no desire to ever return and couldn't understand why anyone else would want to visit. Although we hadn't told her about Jonathan's trip until he was safely home, it would be more difficult for me to simply disappear for ten days. Plus, I didn't want to lie to her.

My concerns about her reaction were not overblown. "How can you do this to me?" she screamed.

I tried to reassure her by explaining that I wasn't going alone, that Frank was coming with me, but this only compounded her horror. "You're taking your *son*! He has *babies*!"

Once she realized I wasn't going to back down, she tried another tactic. She urged me to take a good book and stay in my hotel room.

"There is nothing to see there," she said.

I thought this was going to be her last word on the subject, but she wasn't quite done. When she finally accepted that I was going, she advised me to stay with the group. "Don't do anything stupid," she said.

9

Frank and I had cleared our schedules, given a commitment to the Bet TAL group, and done our homework. Still I kept stalling; I couldn't bring myself to buy our tickets, even though I knew that the longer I waited, the more I would pay.

I was anxious about this trip, even after telling my mother that I was going. In my world of secrets and things unsaid, I was probably also anxious about what else I might find.

In addition to all of this, I am a nervous flier. The choices for airlines that flew into Lviv were limited; I'd never heard of most of the carriers and I was determined to avoid Aeroflot, which I'd flown in the late 1980s out of Leningrad/St. Petersburg. While I obviously lived to tell the story, the bolts meant to secure my seat to the floor of the plane had come loose, and I could feel myself rattling around as we flew.

After researching options, the best choice seemed to be an August 12 Lufthansa flight from Dulles, with a layover in Munich the next day. Now that we had an itinerary for our journey and had learned what we could about the history and geography of these shtetls in Ukraine, it was time to get down to basics: what to actually bring. I tried to pack light, even though I was advised to take extra items, such as toilet paper, soap, and flip-flops for the shower, all of which proved unnecessary. My one luxury—apart from a bunch of granola bars stuffed into my bag—was bringing my own pillow. Whatever else happened, I wanted to be able to sleep well.

Then there was the question of gifts. I wanted to bring something to the family we would be meeting, the one in the photograph. Some suggested I just bring cash, which I did, but that didn't strike me as appropriate. I wanted to give them something tangible—but what? One friend suggested serving utensils, something attractive yet practical that could be used regularly at meals and would remind them of our connection. This struck me as a good idea; I began looking in department stores and on the Internet and finally located some Ralph Lauren pieces that I liked. There was an appealing symbolism: Ralph Lauren is the son of Ashkenazi Jewish immigrants, not to mention an American success story, a man who even designed uniforms for the U.S. Olympic team.

Spoons were meaningful to me for another, more personal reason, as well.

When Sadie, my first grandchild and my mother's first great-grandchild, was born, we talked about what my mother should give her. My mother, a woman who took a pair of scissors and a winter coat with her in the middle of the summer when she fled her shtetl, is above all practical. Her first thought was to give a gift of money, to start saving for the baby's future. I suggested there would be plenty of opportunities to help financially and that she instead find something more meaningful. Together we decided on one of the silver spoons my parents had brought from Germany, a gift rich in both personal and historical terms.

We put one of the silver spoons into a shadow box, along with a picture of me with my parents and a handwritten note from my mother that read: "I brought this silver spoon with me from Europe and am giving it to you, Sadie, with the hope that you will always have a silver spoon in your mouth."

This is a gift she repeated for her eldest grandson, Sasha, as well. While the Ralph Lauren serving spoons were not themselves imbued with this bit of history, they were nonetheless a gift that for me had deep meaning.

I also remembered what Leon Wieseltier had told us, about leaving behind a piece of himself in the shtetl in the form of his book *Kaddish*. I thought about this for a while and decided to bring a batch of our Rosh Hashanah (Jewish New Year) cards. I'd been sending these cards since 1990, inspired by a stranger who offered to take a picture of the five of us when we were dressed up and en route to a wedding at the Mayflower Hotel. I turned that photo into a Rosh Hashanah card and began a tradition going on thirty years, which now includes spouses and grandchildren, with the occasional Photoshop intervention required to remove someone who doesn't belong in the picture. I love looking back at the cards, which chart our family's growth.

I remained incredibly nervous as we flew. It was an overnight flight to Munich, which at least meant I passed much of the time asleep. The rest was spent talking to Frank about what we might expect to find. I had brought a list of places, which we reviewed together, explaining the various names of each shtetl and what we knew of their significance to our family story. We were going to join up with the Bet TAL group in a few days, but we also had our own agenda, which included a visit to my mother's shtetl in Kolki and then meeting the family who had saved my father. Or we hoped it was the family, anyway.

We also discussed a document I had brought outlining how to have someone officially declared a "Righteous Gentile," a designation given to non-Jews who put their own lives at risk in order to help save Jews during the Holocaust. These names are entered into a database at Yad Vashem, where a field of trees has been planted in their honor. Assuming this was the family, I wanted to ensure they received this designation.

I couldn't help but note the irony that we were flying back to our ancestral home on a German carrier—that in fact I had chosen this airline for safety reasons—when it was the Germans who had killed almost all of my family. It also struck me as symbolic that our first stop was Munich, even though we were only transferring flights there: Among the photos I'd packed for this trip was one of a 1947 reunion of Trochenbrod survivors, taken just southwest of this city, at the Foehrenwald Displaced-Persons Camp. My father stands in the

1947 reunion of Trochenbrod survivors, taken at the
Foehrenwalf Displaced-Persons Camp.

center of the photo, wearing his suit and tie. He is between Nachman Roitenberg, whom I met in Israel, and my father's cousin Itzhak Gornstein, who later moved to California and became Izzy Horn.

We landed on time in Munich after a smooth flight, but already there was a potential glitch. Our connecting flight to Lviv did not initially appear to be listed on the departure board, and our query was met with confusion by the clerk at the Lufthansa customer-service desk.

"You mean Tel Aviv?"

"No, *Lviv*," Frank explained. When we showed her the itinerary, she grew puzzled and said she didn't even know that Lufthansa flew there. After a bit of back and forth, we all realized that the city was listed on the departure screen as "Lemberg."

In all of my copious research, I had momentarily forgotten about the various historical names of cities and hadn't accounted for this particular modern-day twist. Lviv has had many different names in the last century, and in the Munich airport, in 2009, it was listed as Lemberg, which is how it was known during the German occupation in World War II and during most of the nineteenth century, when it was on the eastern outskirts of the Austro-Hungarian Empire.

From my window as we were coming into Lviv, I snapped pictures of what looked like serene, lush green farm fields. It was easy to see why Ukraine was often called Europe's "breadbasket" and to forget that it has also been called "the blood lands."

The moment we landed in Lviv after the brief, ninety-minute flight, it was evident that we were far from home. In contrast to the spectacularly modern, chaotic airport from which we had departed in Washington, this terminal, with its turrets and wood paneling, looked like it came from another time. Ours was the only plane on the runway, and uniformed soldiers, in formation on the tarmac, awaited our arrival. It was a clear sign that a journey into western Ukraine, even to one of its largest cities, required a trip back to the nineteenth century.

We were questioned individually about the contents of our luggage. The official questioning me asked how much cash I had on hand. I told him I had two hundred dollars, which was definitely not true, but I had read that was the limit I was allowed to bring. "Only two hundred dollars?" he'd asked. Nervously, I responded, "Do I need more?"

Somehow or other and to our great relief, we made it past customs and found our translator, Anna, and her father, Ivan, waiting for us. They had traveled two and a half hours to pick us up, and now they would take us back to Lutsk, which would be home base.

The highway from Lviv had almost no signs and was riddled with potholes. Cars traveled slowly, in part because many were Soviet-era, but also because the police were always lurking, looking to extract a bribe from someone traveling a kilometer too fast—something we got to see firsthand when Ivan was stopped midway on our journey and had to pay up. I was actually grateful to be moving slowly. It gave us plenty of time to gaze at the perfectly preserved landscape—carts with horses, women selling apples by the road, cows roaming next to bus stops. There was not a hint of globalization, although over the next few days I would begin to see the subtle ways in which the world had in fact encroached.

We had not yet met in person, but Anna and I had been corresponding for well over a year in preparation for this trip. She had spent two summers studying at a school near Panama City, Florida, and her English was good, although she sometimes spoke too quickly for me to understand. She struck me as very businesslike and credible, not prone to sentimentality. As we drove, Frank, ever the historian and journalist, began asking her basic questions to do with the history of the region, but she claimed to know nothing about the past, particularly the past when our family lived in this area.

Whether this was true or she was avoiding potential minefields, she was nevertheless well prepared. She had spent a year working on what she referred to as "the case" and had arranged for us to meet the family in their ancestral village. The entire clan was planning to come, including Mycola—who lived there—and Nadiya, the eldest daughter, who had so far proven to be the most helpful of the bunch, and Victor, the other brother. Anna had been calling Nadiya about once a week, she told us, to coordinate the logistics of this meeting.

Anna told us that the family was "a little embarrassed" by our interest in them and worried that they might say the wrong thing. Nadiya had said, "I wasn't the one who saved their father. Why should they want to see me?" Anna described them as "simple" people who were "not at all spoiled."

She reminded us that she was "ninety percent convinced that they are the family." "When you go into their house and see the photos," she said, "there's not much room for doubt." As had been my posture from the start, I very much wanted to believe her, but I was going to hang on to my skepticism until I could see for myself.

"Why are you only ninety percent sure?" Frank asked her.

"Because this is your judgment and you have to see for yourself," she said. "The last ten percent is up to you."

Ivan, a wiry man of about fifty, worked as an engineer for a local gas company and spoke no English. He seemed as obsessed with our trip as his daughter was and constantly asked her to translate. According to Anna, he had a copy of Jonathan's book; his best friend had given it to him, having found and purchased the only two remaining copies in the Lutsk bookstore. They had just downloaded the movie version, too—the first hint of the sort of postmodernity we would see on this trip, a stark contrast to the ancient landscape.

Frank asked Anna to tell me what she really thought about the book. "It's interesting," was all she said. That's a response I got frequently, even in the United States and Israel.

"You can be honest," Frank told her. "You won't hurt our feelings." She hesitated for a moment, then replied that the book, and the way in which it intertwined real names and places with imagined ones, confused people. But she was nevertheless glad that it had brought attention to what she referred to as "the Problem." This is the phrase that she went on to use on several occasions in reference to the Holocaust. Apparently, not many people in these parts were aware of the magnitude of what happened to Jews living in western Ukraine during the war. It wasn't taught in school and it wasn't discussed.

Our first stop was Lutsk, a fairly sizable city of roughly 200,000, where we would stay in the Hotel Ukraina. It was well located, right near the center of town, and looked like something out of the 1950s, with an avocado-and-gold color scheme, but the rooms were large and clean, which came as a relief. It had been a long couple of days, between the pre-travel anxiety and the long journey, and I pulled out my pillow, hoping to rest before dinner. But almost as soon as I lay down, someone began loudly banging on the door.

Apparently, there had been a mistake and I'd been put in the wrong room; this one was more expensive than what I had booked and prepaid. I was too exhausted to contemplate packing up again and relocating, so I told them I'd stay put and they could bill me the difference. This was easier said than done, I learned. I needed to settle up immediately. Down to the lobby I went, credit card in hand.

Dinner was its own challenge. Neither Frank nor I keep strictly kosher, but we both avoid pork and shellfish. The pork aversion is something my mother instilled in me. It wasn't just the meat itself she was worried about—everything was cooked in lard. One of her repeated admonishments, along with her suggestion that I stay in my hotel room and read, was: "Don't eat *anything* they give you. Bring your own food."

Our first dinner in Lutsk was at a traditional Ukrainian restaurant with Anna, Ivan, Avrom Bendavid-Val, and his wife, Leah, who had arrived early to do advance preparations for the Trochenbroder group.

Frank and I scanned the menu and finally both chose what seemed the safest option, a soup called Vegetable Harmony. After a taste, we exchanged wary glances. There were vegetables, all right, but they were rather unharmoniously afloat in what was almost certainly pork stock. We tried to make light of this by saying we weren't hungry after a couple of polite spoonfuls, but there was no way to avoid upsetting our hosts.

As the rest of the group ate, a three-piece Ukrainian band dressed in embroidered outfits regaled us with nostalgic folk songs about the wonders of this part of the country.

Over dinner I braved the question that, even as a rational person with a strong grasp of history, still concerned me. I was also thinking about Father Desbois's warning that this part of Ukraine was "two hundred percent anti-Semitic." Were we, as Jews, really safe here? I asked. I explained that some American Jews remained fearful of Ukrainians, that they believed they had helped kill their families, that I had been warned this was one of the most anti-Semitic regions in the country. Frank looked at me, rather alarmed, and later told me it was as though I had just thrown a grenade onto the table. Fortunately, the Ukrainians were fascinated by this perception and less upset than I might have predicted. They assured us that we were safe in Lutsk.

We went to bed hungry that night, our bit of soup supplemented by only a couple of granola bars. Fortunately, there would be no more Vegetable Harmony soup for us: Frank and I found a cozy little pizza restaurant in the center of Lutsk, in a place called Rynok Square, where we ate virtually every night that we were on our own. We told ourselves that the pizza didn't contain lard and chose not to explore this theory too closely.

Once the Trochenbroders arrived, we felt less conspicuous in our eating habits; many of them shared our dislike for pork, and the hotel seemed prepared to accommodate. On the portion of the trip when we were alone, without the Trochenbroders, lunch was generally taken care of by Anna, who continued to amaze. She quickly came to understand our dietary restrictions and prepared picnic lunches of hard-boiled eggs and fresh vegetables, for which we were enormously grateful.

Our days in Ukraine were divided into four segments. Frank and I had timed our trip to coincide with the arrival of our fellow Israeli and American Trochenbroders, and with them we would visit the shtetl, or, rather, what was left of the place. On our own, we planned to explore Kolki and Lysche and to meet the family we hoped was the one who hid my father during the war. Then, finally, we would have a couple of days on our own in Lviv, where we could enjoy the comforts of a nice hotel and decompress before heading home.

While Frank and I flew in through Lviv, most of the other Trochenbroders, from both the United States and Israel, flew in to Kiev and met us in Lutsk. One evening, when Frank and I returned from our intimate meal at what we now thought of as our pizza joint, the woman at the front desk of the hotel informed us that a busload of Israelis, accompanied by some Americans, had just arrived from Kiev. She didn't really need to tell us this: They were hard to miss. Seated in the Hotel Ukraina dining room, they were talking at Tel Aviv decibels. It felt as though the Israel Defense Forces had just descended to protect us. Even if they were a noisy bunch, it was comforting to be surrounded by our fellow landsmen, and besides, I was eager to reconnect with Mira and Chaim Binenbaum, whom I'd first met in August 2008, when I brought them the material from our U.S. Trochenbrod gathering and when they guided me from one Trochenbrod survivor to another to learn about my father. Throughout, they had been my touchstone with the Israeli Trochenbroders. Mira and I immediately sat down on the sofa right by the large front window in the Ukraina Hotel lobby to catch up. I told her about all of my new information, which was largely the result of the clues we had picked up when she and Chaim were driving me around Israel the previous year. Based on the discovery that my father had been in Lysche, I'd been able to get Anna and Sergiy to go to the village and find someone who could identify my father and two of the other people in my tattered old picture. I told her how I had continued to work survivor and Holocaust databases but had found no new clues, even knowing the village and that my father's wife's name was Tzipora.

Mira, an expert at these databases, pulled out her computer and tried to figure out other ways to approach the search. So far, I'd been looking through Trochenbrod, Lysche, and Chetvertnia listings. I'd been searching for the names Tzipora, Cipora, or Zipora, and for Safrans. Mostly I was looking for baby Safran.

Frank and Mira huddled together on the sofa as Mira played around with different keywords, until she seemed to find something. Excited, they called me over. She had not found a Tzipora but rather a "Tzipa Kuperschmit"— murdered in 1942 in Zofjówka. We realized that this might actually be her: Survivors call the shtetl Trochenbrod, but it was also known as Zofjówka, Sofiova, Trochimbrod, and several other variations, depending on whether you were talking to a Jew, a Russian, a Pole, or a Ukrainian. Tzipa is, of course, a nickname for Tzipora. But, more important, Kuperschmit was the name of my father's mother, Brucha, after she remarried to Baruch Kuperschmit.

Even more surprising, Mira found that Tzipa's entry listed her husband: Leibel. Leibel *Kuperschmit*. The listing said that he, too, had been murdered in 1942. This seemed to be my father and his wife, but my father was definitely not killed in 1942, although Tzipa and their daughter were. There was no listing for their daughter. And, according to everything we now knew, they hadn't been killed in Trochenbrod or Zofjówka. Digging deeper, we found that the testimonial page had been submitted in 1999 by Noam Rosenblatt, son of Gad and Fanya Rosenblatt, forty-five years after my father killed himself in Washington, D.C.

This made no sense. I could only surmise that there was an attempt to be all-inclusive—that even though Leibel and Tzipa technically lived in another village, they were considered Trochenbroders. But why was my father's name on the list—especially given that in 1947 he stood literally in the middle of the picture of Trochenbrod survivors at their reunion at the Foehrenwald Displaced-Persons Camp? Clearly he had still been alive. And when I visited Fanya Rosenblatt, Gad's wife and Noam's mother, in 2008, she knew my father had killed himself in the United States. Perhaps Gad, who had died about six months earlier, didn't know?

Frank offered a more poignant theory: "Maybe, because of how he died, they still considered him one of the martyrs of the Holocaust."

These somber thoughts were quickly set aside as the head of the Bet TAL group, Moti Litvak, rushed over to Frank and said excitedly, "So you're the hero of Trochenbrod?" He was of course assuming Frank was Jonathan and was referring to *Everything Is Illuminated*, which was in large part responsible for everyone being here. Frank explained that he was Jonathan's brother, and an author himself. Moti seemed unimpressed. "Okay," he said, "so you're the *brother* of the hero of Trochenbrod!"

This was only the beginning of endless comments and questions to do with the book and the movie. We were asked repeatedly, "Why isn't Jonathan here?"

Everyone had something to say about the book. One of our Ukrainian guides asked me to tell Jonathan that, next time, he should tell the *true* story of Trochenbrod. A South American on the trip complained that when he went to a bookstore to purchase a travel guide that included Trochenbrod, he was informed that Trochenbrod was a fictional place created in a novel written by an American.

The confluence of three cultures—Israeli, American, and Ukrainian, with a few South Americans thrown in—produced a fair amount of comedy and tension over the next three days. Our Trochenbrod cousins were warm and entertaining. The shtetl must have been filled with wise guys. Many of them were funny; many more of them *thought* they were funny.

The first day together, before actually going to Trochenbrod, we went on a brief, loosely organized bus tour of the city of Lutsk, with a stop at the official Volyn Regional Archives, where we were given the opportunity to search for family records. Upon arrival, we were sternly lectured by the head of archives: No talking, and no cameras allowed. We were to remain silent or risk ejection. This Soviet-style edict did not take into account the impossibility of quiet in a group that was two-thirds Israeli. They were loud, and they asked not always politely rendered questions when records were not promptly produced. At one point, one of the Ukrainian bureaucrats had enough and began banging her fist on the table. Not much was found in the end, and most of the Trochenbroders walked away disappointed. This was not a satisfying beginning for our group.

Frank and I decided this was a good moment to peel away and walk around the old city of Lutsk by ourselves. It's a city that mixes modernity in the form of Soviet-style offices and apartment houses with the history of an old town, including an ancient castle. Lutsk is where my mother and father first met, and I kept looking around, trying to imagine my parents walking these streets, wondering in which of these buildings they had lived back in 1944. We did manage to find the Choral Synagogue, a small, defensive-looking fortification that is now, of all things, a gym.

After our walk, we returned for dinner with our Trochenbrod landsmen. On the way into the restaurant that night, Betty Gold from Cleveland—the survivor who had written a memoir and whom I had met a year earlier at a Trochenbrod gathering in Washington—introduced us to the Chaitchicks, her cousins who lived in Lutsk. This was fortuitous: My mother had asked me to track down the Chaitchicks, to whom we were remotely related through marriage. This man didn't look like the Chaitchick cousins we are related to. He looked very much Ukrainian, with his mullet haircut, his skin a deep red from the summer sun, and his open shirt with some kind of dangling chain. We talked for a few minutes, with Betty translating, but we never figured out if he was the Chaitchick my mother had wanted me to find. At least I could report the sighting when I returned and check that assignment off my list.

The official business of the trip began that evening. Since we were from four different continents, few of us had previously met, so we all introduced ourselves. After that, Moti Litvak, assisted by Avrom, went over the plan. First we'd take buses to Domashiv, a rural village near Trochenbrod. From there we'd switch to horse-drawn wagons, which would pull us to the site of the old town along the defunct road. Once we arrived in Trochenbrod, Shmuel Potash—a ninety-year-old survivor with a near-photographic memory, who was still going strong—would be able to tell all of us where our families' houses once stood. His father had run the town dairy, and as a child he had delivered milk every morning, which meant he knew—and remembered—the layout well. We would also stop at all of the memorials. Metal from one of the memorials had been recently stolen by locals and sold as scrap, so the Israelis had brought with them large inscribed marble tablets that would, in theory, be impossible to move. I wondered what it must have cost to transport these heavy pieces on El Al from Tel Aviv.

What lay ahead on the itinerary seemed likely to be something of a circus. The next morning, we left the hotel early, en masse, piling onto two modern, large buses. One bus carried the Israelis, the other, the rest of us, including Evgenia Potash, an eighty-eight-year-old survivor who still lived in Lutsk and was presumably related to Shmuel, although I never figured out their exact connection. Evgenia regaled us with stories as we drove. She'd survived by hiding in the woods and had then married a Christian partisan. She let slip that she had a Ukrainian copy of *Everything Is Illuminated* in her studio apartment.

After a long bus trip, we saw people lining the road in Domashiv. It seemed as if the entire village had come out to greet us. It was a scene right out of central casting, complete with babushkas—women with scarves tied tightly around their heads—and older men with caps leaning against fences while children ran around in excitement.

Anna the Translator now took the microphone on the bus to give us some background on the village. Her grandmother was from Domashiv, she said, and she told us that as a child she used to play in Trochenbrod, which by then was no longer a shtetl but simply a place to harvest hay for the winter. They called it the Sofiyevka fields. Sofiyevka was the Russian name for the shtetl. Like Lviv, it had different names depending on who occupied the region.

For many years, people from Domashiv didn't speak of their Jewish neighboring village, except, according to Anna, in occasional sob-filled conversations. Anna's grandmother had been a little girl at play in the fields when she'd heard an unusual commotion. She followed the noise and became an unintentional witness to the mass murder of Trochenbrod.

We'd known we wouldn't be taking the buses into the place that had once been Trochenbrod—there were no real roads. But horse-drawn wagons filled with hay seemed an oddly playful mode of transportation for this solemn tour. We could appreciate the practicality, though.

After a few minutes of hesitation, we departed the buses and headed for the wagons driven by the citizens of Domashiv, many of whom had their young children perched next to them. Anna—who always had an eye out for Frank and me, because we had hired her for the other, private excursions on our trip—picked out a comfortable wagon for us, the carriage padded with a bed of hay. We climbed aboard, like kids on a hayride, and settled in with some of our fellow travelers. Our entourage was brought up in the rear by some of the elderly Trochenbroders, who wisely chose jeeps in lieu of wagons.

Two horses pulled our carriage off the main road and onto a path that took us through the fields. In the background, we could see the flashes of cameras as our fellow Trochenbroders aggressively snapped photos. As if we were not already enough of a spectacle, we were being trailed by a film crew, and a boom mike traveled beside us in another wagon. Our friend and Trochenbroder Jeremy Goldscheider had brought a camera crew to shoot footage for the documentary he was producing on Trochenbrod, this place that was long gone but increasingly well documented.

The Israelis had brought a large Israeli flag, which they unfurled above a wagon farther back in the procession. It was quite a sight, with a half dozen wagons, a film crew, and some jeeps riding through the woods of western Ukraine in search of a Jewish shtetl that no longer existed. One of the local girls in the front seat of our wagon, who was likely the daughter of our driver, decided to follow suit, unfurling the Ukrainian flag, which now fluttered above us. Frank and I found this more than a little disconcerting; I imagined my mother's reaction should she see this, which she probably would, given the number of photographs being taken and the fact that a docu-

mentary film was being made. There were the Trochenbroders on their triumphant return, waving the Israeli flag. And
there was her family, riding under the banner of Ukraine. I
suspected she might not see the humor.

Suddenly the skies above the fields turned gray, and our
hayride came to an abrupt end as it began to pour. We tried
to see the rain as symbolic—we were about to learn that it
had also rained the day after the massacre of the Jews, an at-
mospheric distraction that allowed the few survivors to make
a run for the forest. Still, it was hard to view this downpour as
serendipitous given how wet we were, despite the ponchos
and umbrellas that Anna had thoughtfully brought.

After the wagons turned a corner, we emerged from the
forest into a clearing and saw the first of the four monuments
to the murdered Jews of Trochenbrod—and, to everyone's
relief, someone on the advance team had erected a large tent.
The wagons pulled up as close as possible to the tents and we
all ran in.

Our guides were doing their best, but this group of Trochenbroders wasn't easy, assigning blame all around for having failed to warn the group about the weather. After the
bickering subsided, someone had the idea of handing our
portable microphone to Betty Gold, the seventy-nine-year-
old survivor of the massacre. Betty was what was sometimes
referred to as a "professional survivor." In addition to the
memoir that she wrote, she was a regular on the Holocaust
commemoration circuit, speaking to community and school
groups. On this occasion, however, she was actually here, in
Trochenbrod, telling her story on the very spot where it occurred. Later that day she would visit the site of her childhood home for the last time—she would pass away five years

later. Even though I had read her book and was familiar with her story, hearing it in this context magnified the miracle of her survival.

She was twelve years old in 1942 when the Nazis began knocking on doors, ordering all villagers, including Betty and her grandmother, to leave their homes and walk about two miles to the center of town. Betty didn't see her mother and father anywhere. Terrified, she left her grandmother and managed, astonishingly, to return to her house undetected. When she arrived home, however, her house was empty. She then remembered that her father had been building a wall across the back of a storage shed behind the house. She began banging on the wall, begging to be let in, to no avail. She then started to cry, pleading. At last the wall slid open enough for a hand to emerge, pulling her in. Her parents had hesitated initially, thinking the knocking was the Nazis. Betty stood that night, along with fifteen others, behind that wall, which was about three feet wide. Among those hiding was a woman with a one-and-a-half-year-old child, who began to cry. Terrified they would be discovered, the woman made the harrowing decision to suffocate the baby. When the rain began the next day, her family left, making a run for an underground bunker her father had prepared in the woods. Betty spent the remaining years of the war hungry, foraging for food, convinced of the inevitability of death. Yet she and her family managed to stay alive despite several close brushes. Eventually they joined with Soviet partisans and later wound up at a DP camp.

We listened to Betty as the rain pounded the tent. Once it subsided, we all climbed back into our wet wagons and headed for Trochenbrod's one and only unpaved street, which was actually more like a dirt path. By the time we arrived, the sun was not only out, but the day had turned glorious.

Shmuel Potash now took a megaphone and, like a human GPS system, began to explain where everyone had once lived. He not only knew all the names but had interesting facts and bits of gossip about virtually everyone in Trochenbrod, magically bringing the shtetl alive. In addition, a beautiful map had been put together by the Israeli Trochenbroders, showing where every Trochenbroder had lived; a poster version was given to each family on the trip. I'd been carrying a blueprint of the shtetl in my head, but now I could really see where my grandmother Brucha had lived, which was one house away from her sister-in-law Sosel Bisker and directly across the road from their cousins the Gornsteins. Five houses up, on the same side of the street as my grandmother's house, were other Bisker cousins. A few houses farther up were the Kimelblats. Of course, my father's half sister Choma had married Shai Kimelblat, and by then I had learned that Shai's cousins Natan and Itzhak were my father's partners in Lodz after the war.

Shmuel led the group through Trochenbrod, microphone in hand, delivering a colorful if often hilariously rambling monologue. He had brought twelve members of his family, including children and grandchildren, with him on this trip. He wanted to show them where he came from—in detail. He had a story to go with each house. This guy had been known as Moishe the Fat; this guy was Ellie with a Lump on His Head; this guy loved the ugliest girl in town. He led us through this colorful history as though he were still the little boy delivering the milk.

What made his recollections all the more amazing was how few visual cues remained. Only one tree still stood from the days when Trochenbrod had been a town. After the Germans had torched everything, the Soviets planted new trees and dug canals. The path we were walking along was apparently much narrower than the old road had been. The forest still remained on the horizon and gave the illusion of having been there for decades, but it was in fact all new foliage.

As Shmuel spoke, Betty Gold repeatedly wondered aloud about the whereabouts of her family's former house. Even though this was her third return to Trochenbrod since the war, she found the deconstructed landscape confusing, understandably. As we reached the middle of the street, Shmuel called her to the front of the group and pronounced he had found the spot. Betty walked across brush and stood in waist-high grass and wildflowers. "I never thought I would find this place," she said tearfully. "I never thought I would be here again." She picked a bundle of wildflowers to take back to her home in Cleveland.

Despite the somber reason for our visit, most of our fellow travelers were in good moods, energized by the opportunity to play the role of shtetl archaeologist and look for remains. We even had makeshift tools, and there were, in fact, a few artifacts found. One of the Brazilians had "borrowed" forks from the hotel, which she distributed for people to use as digging tools. And, of course, I had brought a supply of Ziploc bags—enough for everyone.

One of the Americans on the trip, Ethel Kessler, worked beside me as we dug up the broken remains of a plate. Some of the Israeli kids found shards of brick from the old factory. My grandmother Brucha's second husband, Baruch Kuperschmit, had made bricks, and I wondered if perhaps he'd been involved in the creation of some of these. As we dug, one of the locals with us found a token from the old post office, and, according to Shmuel, this was right at the spot where the building had once stood. It seemed *bashert*— destined—that Ethel Kessler, the art director of the U.S. Postal Service, was there with us. The man from Domashiv handed the coin to Avrom, whom he knew from Avrom's previous visits to Trochenbrod and Domashiv. I viewed the coin as the perfect artifact for my glass-jar memory collection. Avrom and I went back and forth for a bit, like kids arguing over a toy, until Avrom's wife intervened on my behalf. I now have the token—an admission I'm not sure I should be proud of, but there it is in my collection, and I cherish it.

Shmuel continued to speak, despite complaints from some of the Israelis in the group, who were growing tired of the way he was monopolizing the microphone. Finally, after about an hour, he ran out of steam and climbed into a jeep to recuperate.

Without Shmuel at the lead, the group was able to quicken its pace, and we made our way to the army surplus tent for lunch. I learned, unsurprisingly, that Frank and I were not alone in our aversion to the standard, pork-heavy Ukrainian diet. Some three-quarters of the group declared themselves vegetarian in an effort to avoid eating the potentially offending meat without insulting our hosts. Betty Gold joked that she could live on bread, which she actually sort of had for about a year while in hiding in the forest. In her memoir, she described sneaking into homes and stealing bread, which was then rationed among her family and the others with whom they were in hiding. Sometimes she would grow so hungry that she couldn't help but pilfer some for herself at night, and then she'd blame it on mice. We all took her cue and raided the breadbaskets.

Seated on benches at long picnic tables inside the tent, bedraggled from the rain, we must have resembled a group of refugees. The Israelis began to lead us in Hebrew folk songs. We all grew emotional and our eyes moistened, not for the first or last time that day.

After lunch, we went to the first of the memorials, which was basically just a plaque that had been installed by the Soviets at the far end of what was once the town.

Then we moved down the path another twenty yards, arriving at the site of the second memorial erected by Trochenbrod survivors—the one that the Israelis planned to restore with the marble they had brought with them from Tel Aviv. Shmuel Potash's grandchildren, wearing white kipot, carefully glued the new plaque in place, as their grandfather, now rejuvenated after his rest, guided them.

The group watched, snapping photos and taking videos. This was why we were here, after all—to keep these memories alive, to ensure that the town was not forgotten, to not allow it to disappear into the Ukrainian landscape of newly planted trees.

Evgenia, the old survivor from Lutsk, pushed her fragile body to the front of the group. "My mother and father died here. I want to say Kaddish," she said.

Shmuel disagreed, insisting that Evgenia's parents had

actually died at another spot, but the crowd managed to silence him.

A Hasidic rabbi suddenly appeared. An apparition in a long black coat, he stepped into the forest next to the memorial. No one was quite sure what he was doing there, but someone must have alerted him to our presence. He explained that he came from Lviv and made it his life's mission to identify mass graves. We later learned that his forensic methodology involved holding two poles above the ground. If they moved, that meant that Jews were buried there. So maybe this was not the most scientific approach, but we were nonetheless relieved to hear him tell us that we were in the right spot. We then commenced readings in both Hebrew and English about Trochenbrod and the Holocaust. Shmuel recited Kaddish for Evgenia's family and for his own, as well as for everyone killed in Trochenbrod.

Betty Gold sat at the base of the memorial and wept uncontrollably. We all looked toward the flag that the Israelis had carried with them to the grave and began to sing the Israeli anthem, "Hatikvah."

As the rest of the group moved on, Frank and I lingered. We wanted to leave behind our family's Rosh Hashanah card. Because we weren't sure which of the memorials marked the spot where our ancestors were buried, we decided to leave our message at every Trochenbroder grave site, of which there were several. We dug a few inches into the ground, placed our family photograph, and covered it with earth.

We then climbed back into our wagon. This time, Avrom rode with us. When we passed through the Yaromel forest, he informed us that we were following the same path the Jews of Trochenbrod had taken when the Germans loaded them into trucks. He knew this from his interviews with Christian villagers.

The Jews arrived at this spot and saw a big pit in the ground, Avrom told us. We knew this story already, of course, and yet with each recounting, history was turning into memory, and memory into history.

They were ordered to remove their clothes and jewelry. The rabbi of Trochenbrod told his flock that they could follow these orders, and he began to disrobe. He was shot before he could finish undressing. The Nazis then ordered the Jews to line up in rows of seven, turn around, and face the pit, where they were shot in the back. As this process was repeated, many made a run for the forest; others went berserk watching. Whether running or standing frozen, screaming, they were all gunned down. When that pit was full, the Nazis moved the remaining Jews to a second site in the forest. These two pits were the sites of the other two memorials. Frank and I buried our family card at each one. We wanted our ancestors to know we were still here.

There was yet another plaque to be reinstalled, this one at the third memorial on our journey.

Here, Shmuel Potash's young Israeli granddaughters set out candles to form a Star of David. A cantor from Washington had brought a guitar, and he played a song he'd written about Trochenbrod. By the time he was finished, even the Israelis, who we thought of as being thick-skinned and tough, were weeping. I was very emotional, too, thinking about my Grandmother Brucha and my Aunt Choma, who might have been murdered on this very spot. A brother and sister from

Argentina who had made aliyah to Israel sang a beautiful song written by a Ukrainian-born Israeli poet, about how "everyone has a name," as the wind blew through the forest and the sun began to fade.

We then sang another round of "Hatikvah," then "Am Yisrael Chai," which translates to "the nation of Israel lives." On this day and in this place, these songs seemed especially meaningful. Despite what had happened here, we lived on as Jews, and as Trochenbroders.

Rejuvenated by these songs, we walked one hundred yards deeper into the woods, past the swelling crowd of Ukrainians that had been following us all day, curious. The next memorial we came upon was also in disrepair, but we didn't have the means to restore it. Shmuel Potash entered the site and instructed his grandchildren to gather around him. His sister, who had survived the massacre, later told him that this was the very spot where his family had been murdered. He wept as he spoke, while a fellow Israeli recited Kaddish. The rest of us hovered nearby, not sure what to say. The sun was beginning to set, and horse-drawn carriages don't have headlights. Finally, the tour leaders insisted that we move along.

After we left the memorial, still in the barren fields of Trochenbrod, a friend of Ivan's was unexpectedly waiting to greet us. He was a tall, thin man, carrying a Russian translation of *Everything Is Illuminated*, one of the two that he had found in the Lutsk bookstore. He was waiting for Frank and me to autograph it. Strange but also oddly fitting. We visited with him for a while and talked about the book.

As we were getting ready to move on, I remembered that we had forgotten to bury our New Year's card at the last grave

site. Frank and I doubled back to the mass grave, alone. We
were in the middle of the forest, where it was cool and quiet.
We noticed a crack in the foot of the memorial and decided
to stuff the glossy evidence of our family's persistence inside
the stone.

The next morning we assembled as a group outside the Hotel
Ukraina for a commemorative photograph—our own version
of the 1947 photo of Trochenbrod survivors. We all hugged,
exchanged contact information, and the buses took off.

10

Frank and I were now on our own, about to embark on the next part of our journey, to Kolki and Lysche.

Frank suggested that each morning before setting off we should meet in his room and he'd interview me, using the new Flip Video camera I had purchased for the trip. We had no particular agenda for these interviews; they just seemed a good way to create a raw transcript of our experience and to capture the minutiae, such as my on-camera announcement that I wanted to change clothes before leaving for Kolki—my mother's shtetl. I'm hardly a fashionista, and in fact I had packed only a couple of pairs of jeans and a handful of shirts, but I didn't feel appropriately dressed for this important occasion. I was going to be with my grandmother Esther, in this place I'd been hearing about my entire life. I don't actually believe I can commune with the dead—or that they can see what I am wearing—but I had heard so much about Esther from my mother and from my grandmother's sisters, Chia and Jean, that I felt deeply connected to her. My grandmother was murdered holding her grandchildren. She died having no idea that one of her daughters, my mother, survived and that there were now numerous generations of descendants. I often wished I could tell her how life turned out for us, and today I would have that opportunity. It was an occasion that at least merited a nicer T-shirt.

Kolki is about thirty miles northeast of Lutsk, along a two-lane road mined with potholes. There are almost no private cars outside Lutsk, only a few trucks, buses, old bicycles, and horse-drawn wagons. The terrain is flat and lush, with farm animals that appear to be roaming freely. If you squint and ignore the poor road conditions, it's possible to imagine you are driving through the American Midwest.

Frank and I were just trying to take it all in, not sure what, exactly, we were looking for. I had brought the map my mother had helped re-create, marking the streets where she and her family had lived and the names and houses of other residents. In addition, Anna had, by a stroke of good luck, cousins who lived there and had agreed to be our emissaries.

We also had the name of the Christian family who had provided food and shelter for my mother when she returned after the war, when she learned that her family had been massacred. The Christian family that had offered her food, which she'd refused even though she was hungry: *If nothing matters, then there is nothing to save.* The simple act of faith that had become part of our family legend.

We were also looking for the remains of a small vegetable oil factory near the river, which had been the backyard of the home where she had lived with her mother and her sister, Pesha. We knew the house itself was gone—my mother had discovered this when she'd returned in 1944 to find only the metallic foundations of the oil factory and to see someone walking on the other side of the street in a dress that had belonged to her older half sister, Lifsha.

From what we knew of Kolki, it appeared to be remarkably unchanged. There was still no indoor plumbing, and the houses were similar in style to how they had appeared in my mother's day, from what I could see and what I knew from the descriptions she had given in the audiotaped interviews. The same breeds of livestock still lived next to the houses, lending the whiff of manure. Everything appeared much as my mother had described: the same swampy paths, the same horse-drawn tractors. This was an illusion, of course. It's not as though the place had been untouched. During the war, the entire village had been torched, first the Jewish part, then the rest. The only house that remained was owned by a German family. Then the entire village had been rebuilt in much the same style as before the war.

Frank said it was as though Ukraine was collapsed in time, that what had happened seventy years earlier could have happened yesterday—or today.

Anna's young cousin decided that it would be best to begin our inquiries by visiting with his high school teacher Anna Gaponjuck. He wanted to make the introduction himself, before heading off to work, so our first stop—after pausing to take a photograph by the town sign—was to pick him up and drive to his teacher's house.

The knock on the door was answered by a woman in her seventies. I'm not sure what I expected, but I couldn't have anticipated Anna, a charming live wire in a leopard-print dress, with hair pulled into a neat bun. She gave us a warm welcome, plying us with candy that a friend had recently brought from St. Petersburg. The place was a bit chaotic, strewn with papers and boxes as well as lots of small hand-made rugs and doilies.

She knew what we were after and didn't waste any time:

"I remember seeing blood on the ground," she told us. She'd been only five when the massacre occurred, and her story unfolded in haunting fragments. She recalled that her father had been ordered to transport clothing back from the freshly dug massive grave site. After doing it once, he refused to continue. "My mother went to the Ukrainian policeman and pleaded, 'I'm pregnant and about to give birth. Don't send him back.'"

She also remembered seeing a man run from the site, and he then hid in their bushes. "Because we had eight children and we were afraid to get killed, we didn't let him stay long," she explained.

As she spoke, her husband, who was rail-thin, entered the room and, squatting against the wall, offered his own memories. "I saw a Jew throw salt in the eyes of soldiers and try to run from them," he said. "It didn't work." I had heard this same story from my mother years before.

Anna the Teacher spoke in such a rapid-fire manner that even Anna the Translator, who spoke very quickly herself, couldn't make sense of everything she said. But we were able to get the gist of her story.

When the Germans torched her family's house, she said,

she and her family fled to the forest and lived in a bunker for six months, right next to the Jewish mass grave.

After we spoke for a while, absorbing these stories, I showed them some of the photographs that I'd brought. I had photographs of my mother, her parents and grandparents, and hoped that someone would recognize them. She didn't recognize anyone but suggested we talk to the older people who lived across the road.

We agreed, and we all walked across the street and knocked on the door. We were greeted by an elderly couple. The man was missing a couple of fingers on one hand, was unshaven, and had no control of his drooping tongue. His wife, who was blind, wore a scarf tightly tied around her head. The house was a mess: The front room was lined with chairs that appeared to have been salvaged from an auditorium.

There was something horribly depressing and uncomfortable about this, but we were here and perhaps they could help. I recited some of the names that I remembered my mother mentioning, as well as ones that appeared on our homemade map. Their faces were blank until I landed on the name Averbuch, who my mother told me had been the town photographer. This rang a bell, and the man retrieved an old photo album and began to flip through it. He couldn't find this Averbuch person, but the old photos stirred up other memories, though nothing especially useful for us. He'd been twenty years old in 1941, he told us, and he claimed to have been out of town during the massacre. He would have been about the same age as my mother and may have even gone to school with her. No matter what we asked, he insisted he didn't remember anything, that he hadn't even been in Kolki at the time.

Anna the Teacher sensed this encounter wasn't going especially well and announced, diplomatically, that it was time to leave. We were now going to visit the mass grave, she said, as if she had just checked the itinerary and we had slipped off schedule. We were happy to let her guide us, even though this was not part of the plan. But she seemed genuinely interested in our search and committed to getting us results.

We went back to her house, and she asked us to wait while she changed out of the leopard-print dress and into something more somber, which she accessorized with a large straw hat. This visit to the mass grave was clearly, for her as well as for us, a serious and important affair. Out of the corner of my eye I could see her applying lipstick. She then went into her yard and cut flowers, which she wrapped in a sheet of cellophane and tied with a ribbon.

We all climbed into Ivan's van and off we went, although where, exactly, we were headed we didn't quite know, other than that we needed to drive disconcertingly deep into the forest—the same forest my mother and Sura were afraid to walk through to say Kaddish. We were basically in the same boat Jonathan had been in eleven years before; he had told us that no one in Kolki knew where the mass grave was, until someone remembered the people who had come to dig for gold teeth—a disturbing thought in its own right, never mind the coda that once they were in the forest, he'd feared they'd never find their way out.

Anna the Teacher didn't know where to begin, either. Anna the Translator had been there once before, when she was doing advance work for our trip; she'd found the grave site and had sent me a photograph, but she now couldn't remember the way. As we drove around, we found a villager and asked him for directions. Like nearly everyone we encountered, he was curious about what a couple of Americans were doing in Kolki and wanted to be part of the adventure. He was determined to show us the way and, rather than explain, he climbed into the van. Our growing entourage now included this helpful villager, Anna the Teacher, Anna the Translator, Ivan the Driver, Frank, and me. The villager seemed to actually know the way, directing us past a herd of cows, then into the forest and off the dirt road onto a path, until we found the spot.

The memorial, erected by some Kolki survivors, was a black slab of stone on a moss-and-weed-covered mound, beneath which lay several thousand bodies. The ground was covered with soft clay, which the villager explained was meant to help prevent the spread of infection from the bodies beneath. At the base of the stone, someone had left plastic flowers, which were now covered with cobwebs.

Anna the Teacher was the first to approach. She set down her freshly cut flowers and began to pull the weeds. She was clearly embarrassed by the poor upkeep. "I will call the town council," she announced. "The condition of this site is a scandal." She was then joined by the rest of our group, and someone translated the inscription, which turned out to be somewhat uninspired. It simply explained that "four thousand brave Soviet Jews" had been killed.

Here I was at last, standing on the grave of my grandmother, my great-grandmother, aunts, cousins, and countless other murdered members of my family. The Ukrainians kindly backed away, giving us space, but what we wanted was a bit of real privacy for this moment. Frank and I walked around to the other side of the monument, where the slab provided a partial shield. I took out a kippah, a traditional head covering worn during prayer, for Frank; a copy of the Kaddish, the memorial prayer; and one of our Rosh Hashanah family photo cards. I handed the card to Frank, and he tried to find a crack in the surface so he could stuff the photo inside, as we had done at the memorials in Trochenbrod. When that didn't work, we put the card on the ground and covered it with earth. I then placed a large stone on the base of the grave, which is an old Jewish tradition: Flowers on graves fade, whereas stones represent the permanence of memory. We recited Kaddish in this sacred place and began to weep.

The moment was surreal. This was the place I saw when I bolted awake at night, imagining my grandmother and great-grandmother holding my cousins in their arms, standing by the pit, waiting to be shot. As my feet sank into the soft clay, I imagined myself moving closer to their bodies. I tried not to think about how deep into the forest we were, about the grave robbers Jonathan had mentioned, about the story we had just heard from Anna the Teacher involving snipers who had perched in the trees, taking aim at would-be escapees. About the descriptions I'd heard from Father Desbois, about how the ground had continued to move for several days after the executions.

Frank told me later that he will never forget being in the dark, peaceful forest, where he said he could feel the ghosts hiding behind the trees.

It was a place of unimaginable horror, but now it was strangely tranquil. Trees had grown on top of the graves, and, in contrast to the noisy village clamor, the sounds of cars and barking dogs, here there was silence.

I imagined my family—not only their deaths but also the lives they had led in this very same town:

On the Sabbath, there was chicken, beef sometimes, turkey maybe twice a year for the big holidays. . . . Schmaltz was a big thing . . . they used to beg the butcher should give them a little bit of fat.

Being here made it so much more real. How I wished they could see all the good that came later: the births, bar mitzvahs, the graduations and weddings, the great- and great-great grandchildren.

I scooped some dirt and pine cones into my Ziploc bag and filled it to the brim. We then pulled ourselves together and made our way back to the van.

"That must be hard. I'm so sorry," Anna the Translator said. "What happened to you people was horrible." The ride back from the mass grave was respectfully silent, for which we were grateful.

After we dropped off the villager, Anna the Teacher resumed her role as guide. She seemed determined to help us find something.

She took us to some of the oldest houses in town. These had not been Jewish houses, and while interesting to see, a tour of historic homes was not really what we were after. But, as I was learning, often you don't know what you are looking for until you find it.

Once again, a local man emerged from his small wooden house, curious to know who we were. We showed him the photos of my mother, of my grandparents, of my aunts, and of my cousins, to no avail. We had just begun to walk away when we heard him say the name "Spitz," pointing to the house on the corner. Spitz was a name that my mother had mentioned as being a neighbor of her grandparents, and it was one of the names on the map that my mother and I had drawn together. We asked if the man remembered anyone named Bronstein, which was the surname of my mother's grandparents, my great-grandparents, who lived near Spitz. They had some sort of mill in their backyard, I told him. Although he didn't recognize the name, he remembered there had been a mill down the street from the Spitz home.

He led us through a backyard, over a fence, into another backyard, and then through crops and over heaps of dung. Another couple of villagers appeared, kindly handing us pears they'd just picked. Our entourage continued to grow, all of them debating which Jew had lived in which house. They had all been children during the war, which meant their memories were imprecise. Despite their desire to help, this was all beginning to feel rather hopeless. And yet memories were being jogged, and suddenly someone said, "There was a flour mill here . . . this is where the Roismans lived."

This was pay dirt. Roisman was the married name of my mother's aunt, whose maiden name was Bronstein. She was my grandfather's sister, who had lived in the same house as my mother's grandparents—which is to say, this was my great-grandparents' house. These villagers, who were children at the time of the war, didn't remember the oldest generation in the house; they remembered the next generation who lived there—my mother's Aunt Sosel, her husband, Shlomo, and their four children, Shmuel, Maya, Moshe, and Chia. I have one picture of my Great-Aunt Sosel and her family, but I didn't think to bring it. This was clearly the same house my mother talked about all the time. It was one of the biggest houses in Kolki—the first one to have electricity, and even a piano. This was the house that my Aunt Pesha would run to on Friday afternoon to bring challah my grandmother Esther had baked for Lifsha and her family, who also lived in the house. I was standing on the very spot where my great-grandparents had lived, along with their extended family.

"This old guy didn't want to leave his house when the Germans came," someone said, pointing to the house. They seemed to be referring, of course, to my Great-Grandfather Nissan. "He told them, 'I'm not going with you,' so they shot him on the spot." Now we knew why my mother's grandfather had never been in the ghetto.

This discovery gave us renewed energy. Someone suggested we go down another street, where other Jews had lived. One thing led to another; the name Chaitchick came up, and we wound up being led down a street called Chaitchick, which was another name on my mother's map—she had lived across the street from them. Her Aunt Ethel had married one of the Chaitchicks. This meant that my mother's house—or, at least, the site of what had once been her house—had to be here.

We then learned of an interesting glitch from one of our impromptu guides: When Kolki had been rebuilt after the war, apparently everything was scrambled, put back together again on a slightly different grid. Even the Styr River, the once timeless navigational guide, had been dammed and re-directed by the Soviets. It was impossible for anyone to get their bearings.

That's when yet another old man appeared on the scene. His name was Ivan—we now had two Ivans and two Annas in our group. Coincidentally, this Ivan had been recommended as a source by Anna the Translator's cousin, with the caveat that he had difficulty hearing and we would have to shout to be heard. He was here to check out the commotion, and to set us right.

"You've got it all wrong," he explained. "The Chaitchick house was on a different corner of Chaitchick Street. It's over there."

He was certain, he told us. The house across the street had belonged to a woman who lived there with her two daughters. One of these daughters, he said, had mysteriously disappeared just as the Germans entered town. This same daughter reappeared after the war for one night and then left again. He had heard this story as a boy. And he was, unbeknownst to him, describing my mother, her mother, and her sister, Pesha.

I could barely breathe, staring at what I now knew to be the exact spot where my mother had grown up.

We followed him to the Chaitchick house on a different corner of Chaitchick Street and entered through a gate across the road to what must have been my mother's old yard. He rattled the door of the house that now stood there, and when no one answered, we walked around to the backyard. We took it all in for a moment, including the satellite dish on the roof. Suddenly a young man emerged, looking at us suspiciously; moments later, his wife and baby appeared beside him. He was clearly not happy to have these foreign strangers standing in his yard, and I got the sense, as we'd been warned, that he was suspicious of us, that perhaps he thought we'd come to reclaim our land. With an eye toward defusing the situation, I began to play with the chubby, adorable baby, and I asked if I could take her picture. After a time, he could see that we came in peace, and he began to soften.

My mother used to tell me stories about how her house had led to the Styr River, so we all walked down to the riverbank to see for ourselves. I thought about the man in the canoe, the dentist who had called on her a couple of times— the character who appeared in her stories more frequently than perhaps she realized. The river was also the place where the Jews would go to clean their dishes before Passover, in preparation for the seder. The place where, on Shabbat, families would stroll along its banks.

The Soviets may have reengineered the river, but its serenity remained unchanged. Ducks swam in formation; a boy cast a fishing line; canoes still lined the banks.

Frank said it was here that, for the first time, he could envision his grandmother leading a happy life, a "normal life." It was peaceful and oddly beautiful and not difficult to imagine my mother here, a teenager with boyfriends.

I wanted to linger for a while, but by this point we had become quite the spectacle, and Frank and I decided it would be best to return on another day, when we could walk in Kolki alone. We needed time to just absorb this place, to breathe and let our imaginations roam.

That night, we went to Shabbat services in Lutsk. Coincidentally, the man who ran the shul was the grandchild of Trochenbrod survivor Evgenia Potash, who was with us on our trip to Trochenbrod. Evgenia had married a Christian Ukrainian partisan and stayed in Lutsk. Now her grandson not only led the small community of Jews but was about to leave to study in Israel for a year. Nobody in the service spoke either Yiddish or English. They probably wanted to be warm to us, but I got the sense that Ukrainian Jews, who were mostly transplants from Russia, had a natural suspicion of outsiders encroaching on their religious observances. Perhaps this was because the congregants were mostly women, and they had come of age before the fall of the Soviet Union, when a service like this would have been verboten.

They sang with real passion, accompanied by a taped recording of Shabbat melodies. The fact that they probably all came to religious observance late in life made it all the more stirring. We tried to be inconspicuous, sitting in the back of the room by ourselves, and we left quietly after the service. Even if we had not been able to communicate with anyone, we were still glad to have celebrated Shabbat in Lutsk, the city where my parents met after the war.

The next day we wanted to return to Kolki without the entourage. We asked Anna and Ivan to deposit us on the old Jewish main street in Kolki—a place memorialized in a 1937 photo of my grandmother, Aunt Lifsha, Great-Aunt Sosel, and Great-Aunt Necha, who had been visiting from St. Louis. They were arm in arm, laughing gaily, looking very stylish, dressed for the Sabbath in their high heels and dresses. It was somewhat hard to imagine them walking these streets looking so fashionable, given the current desolation of the place.

I wondered what might have been had the Jews remained. How would the place have changed? Would it have developed differently? More rapidly? Or would it have been just the same? What becomes of a community when it loses an entire group that had once been integral to the population? Or, as in any rural area in any country, would those with ambition have fled to the big city, or even abroad to the United States and Brazil, as some of my family did in the early 1900s?

We went back to the fallow field where my great-grandparents' house once stood, now covered in rich black manure. Although all of the houses around it had been re-built, their lot remained empty. I paced from one end of the field to the other, trying to imagine their house and their life. I'd always had the narrative, but this was the first time that I had the setting; now I could actually locate the street my Aunt Pesha had walked as a teenager when she visited my Aunt Lifsha and her family, carrying freshly baked challah. I could almost hear the music coming from the piano and smell the challah.

Less happily, I could now see Pesha running down the same street, pressing on my mother the pair of shoes she was wearing.

Frank and I walked for a while, until we crossed a bridge over a marsh and made our way to the place where my mother's house once stood. I snapped dozens of pictures, even though I felt awkward fetishizing a building that she'd never occupied and that now belonged to someone else, with no connection to our story. Still, this was where she had grown up.

For a few minutes, Frank and I said nothing to each other. There wasn't much to say: There was an almost spiritual quality to this trip, a suspension of reality. Sometimes we felt bad for not feeling worse. There was a lot to process, and some of it was going to take a while to sink in.

Then we walked down to the river again, to take it in one last time. I scooped some sand and a few small shells from the shore to take home in my Ziploc bag.

———

The next morning we made another visit to Anna the Teacher. She had insisted that we come back the next day. The prospect of our return had clearly produced a flurry of work. She had moved her sofa to a new spot and hung tapestries. She had also apparently just milked the cow. She wanted to serve us fresh, warm, unpasteurized Kolki milk, which she brought to us in a jug, pantomiming how she had squeezed the udders. In addition to milk, she brought a bowl of cheese curds, sugar, and two jars of sour cream to demonstrate how to make cottage cheese. She then retrieved yet another bowl, this one containing dozens of small potato pancakes, which she slathered with the freshly made sour cream.

Don't eat anything they give you.

Truly there was no polite way out of this one. Anna the Teacher had clearly put a lot of effort into preparing this feast, and Anna the Translator was telling us what we already knew, that we would disappoint our host if we didn't eat—even though we couldn't help but notice that neither Anna nor her father partook.

Somehow, we managed to consume the meal, which Ivan captured, for better or worse, on video. After this generous display of food, Anna the Teacher began to ply us with gifts. First, a colorful, handmade crochet doily. I said it was beautiful—which it was—and marveled at her handiwork. She then grabbed a bag that she had sewn and insisted I take it. I tried to find the right balance between complimenting her and not encouraging her to present us with more gifts, but I was clearly failing. Next, she took off her homemade ruffled apron and shoved that into the bag, too. She then went to her garden and retrieved tomatoes and peppers, which she added to our stash.

Our next stop was the remote village of Kolikovich, the town where my Grandmother Esther, my Great-Aunt Jean, Great-Uncle Jose, and their siblings were born. Kolikovich was really a dorf. It was, quite literally, at the end of the road—a bumpy, unpaved road at that. Behind the village was nothing but forest. My mother had told us not to bother going there: "It's such a nothing place," she'd said. And she was right. This nothing place didn't even have a sign. But that was beside the point. This was the site of more stories for me, and very vivid ones.

There was the story of Uncle Jose—or Itzhak the Shoeless, as he'd apparently been known around here—who had left for Brazil while still in his teens to meet up with his older brother, Solomon. Jose, as he was called in Brazil, ultimately became a major coffee grower and was on the board of the largest bank in South America—coming from this "nothing place." He was the fourth of my great-grandmother's children to leave. She'd been so despondent that she apparently ran after the wagon that carried him away. It was hard to imagine this nothing place containing a personality the size of Aunt Jean or Itzhak/Jose. Frank and I mused about what it must be like to leave a spot such as this, at the end of the road, at the end of the world. How could you even begin to imagine what life must be like elsewhere, in places like Lutsk or São Paulo or Washington, D.C.?

On our way out of town, Ivan stopped the car and sprang out. We watched for a moment, confused, as he grabbed a rock and used it to write "Kolikovich" in the dirt. He had made us a sign against which to pose, and he snapped our picture for posterity.

Outside Kolki, Ivan made an unexpected detour, one that startled us at first: He headed back into the forest, not far from the mass grave. Ivan, it turned out, was a forager, and he wanted us to see the impressive variety of wild berries and mushrooms in these parts. Drying and exporting mushrooms had been my grandfather's trade, as well. It was the business that made it possible for him to have that big house in Kolki, the one with a piano and electricity, and the reason he traveled back and forth to the United States.

Much had changed in Kolki. The Jews were gone. The river had switched course. Satellite dishes adorned the roofs. And yet the place was, in more ways than not, largely untouched. The constancy of mushrooms, at least, was a strange comfort.

11

We were on to the most anticipated part of the trip—to Lysche, or Krynychne, as it was now called, where we would meet the grandchildren of Davyd Zhuvniruck, the man who may have hidden my father during the war.

Anna briefed us about the family. Some of this we already knew: The ancestral house in Lysche, also known as Lyszceze, and now called Krynychne, belonged to the middle grandchild, Mycola. Nadiya, a nurse, was the eldest child and the one who had organized today's events. One of her children was a computer programmer in Lutsk. The youngest brother, Victor, was a physics teacher, who unexpectedly had to work that day, so he'd dispatched his wife and two daughters instead.

It was easy to simply fold this information into the itinerary: Today we would rise, eat breakfast, take a road trip, and meet the family. But when I stepped back to think about it, what lay ahead was surreal. Assuming that the last 10 percent added up, that this was really the family that hid my father—well, I'd been quite literally dreaming of this day much of my adult life.

After a drive of about one hour, Anna called Nadiya to let her know we were nearby. The entire family poured out of the house to greet us on the road. When we hugged Nadiya and Mycola, they embraced us for an extra beat or two, or so it seemed—we were so primed to find deep meaning in every gesture and in every word, we probably needed to calm down and take a few deep breaths.

Nadiya was sixty years old, a slim and stylish woman dressed in gray slacks and a gray turtleneck sweater with her hair pulled tightly into a bun. She was not entirely what I'd expected to find in this desolate town. The first thing she did was lead us to the field in back of the house, shooing away a dog, weaving through roaming poultry, and crossing over weedy mounds that once nurtured potatoes. She had grown up here, the place where Mycola still lived. She wanted to show us where their family house had stood during the war, which was about one hundred feet behind the current house and farther back from the dirt road, where it would have been easier to hide someone.

There was nothing there now. According to Nadiya, the pear tree in the yard was the only thing that remained from before the war. The Jews were all gone—murdered or, in a few rare instances, escaped, and their houses destroyed. A few dozen houses lined each side of the road, and behind them were fields that bled into the forest. But that was about it. This pear tree in the yard appeared to be the only survivor, and it continued, with a ripe symbolism, to bear fruit.

I may have gone a bit overboard with the metaphor, but to me this pear tree symbolized life, and more life. Trees regenerate. They are sometimes capable of growth even after decimation, as was the case with this tree. Everything around it had burned, but there it was, still: the roots, the trunk, the leaves, the fruit, and even the shade.

I imagined my father and his family eating pears from this tree, and that naturally led me to pull out a Ziploc and stuff it with leaves. I also took a possibly excessive number of photographs, including one of us with our Ukrainian hosts posing in front of the tree. They all watched, smiling politely, surely wondering why this crazy American woman was so obsessed with a tree.

In Ukraine. The descendants of the family that hid my father during the war, with Frank and me.

After the photo session, we headed to the house and entered through the back door. I felt as though I had fallen into some time-bending wormhole. The first thing I saw was an old-fashioned woodburning stove. It looked similar to the one my mother had described from her house, yet tinier and even more antiquated than she'd been able to convey, with a brick oven built into the wall just above it.

Sepia and black-and-white photos lined the walls of the living room, many of them hung weirdly close to the ceiling. Nadiya had to step onto a chair to reach one of Davyd and his wife, Yaryna, and we all crowded in for a closer look. I noticed that he was wearing a necktie, and I remembered what the FBI agent had told me about paying close attention to possible similarities in clothing. I asked Nadiya about the tie, and she told me that the picture was a "cut and paste," which was to say the pre-Photoshop way of transposing her grandfather's head onto the shoulders from a different photograph. "He never wore neckties," she explained. Then she went on to casually mention that he liked to wear shirts with two buttons at the top. "My grandmother and then my mother made the shirts for him," she added.

Nadiya took the photo that I had brought of my father and Davyd and studied it for a moment, then said, "This is the type of shirt that I remember well. This is the type that he liked to wear that my mother made." Then Nadiya pulled out another photo of her grandfather, with her and one of her brothers—Davyd was wearing the Nehru-like high-collar shirt with buttons. This is exactly what the FBI agent told me: These people didn't have large wardrobes and had likely worn the same thing in pictures.

Could this be real? Could this really be the family we were searching for? I stopped and held my breath, not knowing what to say, wanting to be convinced but somehow still not allowing myself to be 100 percent certain.

After we looked at the photographs, Nadiya insisted that we all take a seat, even though Mycola was eager to fetch an old woman who lived down the street; she had known his grandfather, and he believed she might be able to help us piece things together. But Nadiya was clearly the one in charge, and she talked right over him. Spunky and straightforward, with a loud, gravelly voice, she provided us with tantalizing snippets of memory from her childhood. I was so eager to hear all of this that I imagined stuffing everything she said into a Ziploc, lining up her words on my mantelpiece at home.

I asked Nadiya to tell us about her grandfather Davyd. She said he never talked much and that he said very little about this period of his life, but she was able to provide some raw facts. He was born in 1900 and died in 1978. He'd been a religious man, a member of the Ukrainian Orthodox church, and on the rare occasions that a priest couldn't make it to the village, he'd step in. She said his grammar was excellent, and, unlike many others in town, he could read and write. He had cows and horses and owned fields across the street from the house. She said that he never drank, never smoked, and never argued. When he did something, he insisted that it be done right.

He had four children, two of whom were still alive but not living locally. One of his daughters had become a judge. He was evidently buried nearby, and I wish I had thought to visit his grave.

There were several stories that had clearly stuck with Nadiya since childhood. On one occasion, she explained, her Uncle Feder was visiting his parents and siblings. Nadiya was about ten years old, and she'd been hiding, eavesdropping on the conversation. She overheard Feder recall how lucky they'd been when German invaders burst into the house and failed to notice the man they were hiding behind the door. "The whole family could have been killed," she remembered her uncle saying. According to my mother, who I suppose had heard this story from my father, these children would take turns playing outside, watching the house to alert the family if the Germans were approaching.

Nadiya also elaborated on a cryptic comment she'd overheard about how her mother should have married Leibel. When she was in seventh grade, her family had just started building a house, she said, and finances were tight. One day, the kids wanted candy, and her mother pressed their father for a little money. Their father was drunk and became extremely surly. "You should have married Leibel if you wanted to be rich," he told her. Nadiya hadn't known what that was about, but she assumed that Leibel was her mother's ex-boyfriend.

This was definitely adding up: I'd already heard from my mother that after the war, Davyd had gone to Lutsk to find Leibel and that he'd urged him to come back to the village and marry his daughter Katarina.

I could have stopped here and drawn my conclusions, but I pressed a bit further. The ultimate proof that this was the family would be to find a copy of the same picture that I had brought. Surely, they, too, had this photograph of my father with Davyd and Katarina. But Nadiya said these were all the pictures they had. She told us the story about her mother putting a bunch of photographs inside the drawer of an old wooden table and setting it on fire, which we had heard before, from Anna. It seemed my last 10 percent proof might have gone up in flames years ago.

We asked more questions about the house, prompting Nadiya to describe the layout of their original house. She explained how easy it would have been for Leibel to sneak out through the back door and hide in the hay in the barn. I asked her to draw a floor plan in my notebook, which she did, and agreed it would have been ideal for hiding someone.

Mycola mentioned the old lady again, suggesting she might be able to shed additional light on this. When he got no response from his sister, he decided to just go out and fetch her himself.

Meanwhile, Nadiya asked us a simple question that went straight to the heart of the matter: "Why are you here?"

Why *were* we there? Of course, we knew the answer—we wanted to see where our family had come from and to find the family that had saved my father—but, also, what were we really hoping to find?

We replied that we knew little about Leibel and hoped to fill in this hole in our family knowledge. History is part luck, part contingency, we said: It was our luck that Leibel turned to their family for help, because it is the contingent fact without which we wouldn't exist. Nadiya got this.

Her understanding seemed to stop, however, when in my excitement I started to tell her about Jonathan's book, going all the way back to how it had begun as a senior thesis at Princeton University. They were unfazed as I continued, explaining that a version of *their life story* had been turned into a movie. I didn't even get much of a rise when I said that the movie starred a guy from *The Lord of the Rings*.

They were not impressed by this Hollywood connection, but they were intrigued by the family New Year's card that I showed them, the same one that we had buried in all of the mass graves. Nadiya asked me to annotate it carefully—she wanted to know who everyone was, both their names and their relations to the rest of the family. I got the sense that they would keep that card for the rest of their lives, that it wouldn't be set on fire inside a desk drawer.

Now that I was feeling this deep connection, I perhaps too boldly jumped to the subject of having their grandfather declared a Righteous Gentile at Yad Vashem. Excitedly, I explained that they might even get an expenses-paid trip to Israel to attend the ceremony. I clarified that this wouldn't be a religious ceremony—it was entirely about preserving and honoring history. Nadiya appeared completely uninterested. "We are simple people," she said. "We've never been abroad. It would be too much for us. But if you want to do something, go ahead. It's up to you."

I could see that in my enthusiasm, I had rushed this idea; it was too much to suggest on this occasion.

Shortly after Nadiya left the room to prepare lunch, Mycola returned with the old lady, whose name was Anna Gorynovich. This new Anna—we now had met three Annas—was surprisingly large, with thick hands and fingers that were twisted from age, or from arthritis, or from years of hard work. She wore a scarf around her head and had no teeth. With each sentence, it seemed she was expending what little remained of her dwindling lung capacity.

Anna the Old Lady, as she came to be known in our Anna-filled lexicon, looked at the picture and instantly identified Davyd and Leibel. She looked at us in confusion, until Mycola explained who we were. Her reaction was immediate.

She came right over to Frank and put her hand to his brow and told him that he had many of his grandfather's features. This was not the first time we'd heard this—the same thing had happened in Brazil, when Itzhak had felt Frank's eyebrows and said they reminded him of Leibel's. Anna then picked up the photograph that I'd brought and said that the woman in the front row was indeed Nadiya's and Mycola's mother, Katarina. She wasn't sure who the second woman in the photo was.

I leaned over to Frank and asked him whether he was convinced we'd found "the family."

"One hundred and ten percent," he whispered.

Anna began to recount some of the history, which I recorded in a notebook. She told us that Leibel had been Davyd's neighbor. In fact, we were sitting on the very spot where Leibel's house once stood. His living room had been right here, right where we were now sitting. Then she described the details of the house: It was made of white wood, with walls of clay. The roof wasn't thatched, like most, but made of metal material. And she said that the windows were long, not square. It was amazing to me that she could remember so many specific details. Here I was, in the very space where my father and his family lived, able to visualize it.

Anna the Old Lady went on to tell us that Jews and Christians got along well in this small town. Her own father, she said, had even spoken some Yiddish. Without prompting, she began to tell us about religious life in the village. There was a house where Jews would pray every Saturday, on Shabbat. When the rabbi came, he arrived on a fine horse. During the week, the men wrapped their arms with leather straps, presumably tefillin (phylacteries).

There were personal details, too. She told us that my father's wife's name was Tzipa, or Tzipora, and that she was an excellent seamstress. That's exactly what Fanya Rosenblatt, who lived nearby, had told me the previous year in Israel. Tzipora was known for her elaborately embroidered designs. Leibel, she said, owned a shop and traveled around the area, selling and buying merchandise.

Then she offered a piece of information that didn't match up to the history that I thought I knew. She told us that Leibel's father had been called Yosso Voskoboy. The first part of his name sounded sort of right—we knew he was Yosef. We were confused by Voskoboy, but it was apparently a nickname with an obscure origin: If kids didn't know how to solve a problem in school, Yosso Voskoboy would come and help them, which was to say he was smart. Sure, we'd happily claim the smart part, but, still, something wasn't lining up. I'd always thought my father's mother, Brucha, was a widow who had lived in Trochenbrod, then later remarried and had another child, Choma—my father's half sister. I was so excited by all of the other revelations, however, that I decided to overlook this one anomalous bit, that my grandfather had still been alive in the village. As I continued to think about it, only one answer made sense.

Several years later, when Frank was in Rio, I asked him to meet again with Itzhak Kimelblat. I wanted to ask him if it was possible that my grandparents had divorced, which was the only logical explanation. Itzhak told Frank that my guess was right. My grandmother Brucha had divorced Yosef and later married Baruch Kuperschmit, the guy with the brick factory who was deaf and had come from a big Trochenbrod family. I suppose it shouldn't have been surprising that life was complicated, even back then.

Anna went on to tell us about how the Germans had kept Jews in the ghetto in Chetvertnia well after they had already killed most of the Jews of Kolki and Trochenbrod. It was such a small town off the main road that they could have easily missed it, but of course we knew they didn't. At first, she said, the Germans rounded up the Jews and sent them in trucks to a ghetto in the small town nearby called Chetvertnia. According to Anna, the Jews were ordered to put yellow circles on their backs, presumably with the Star of David, as had happened in other ghettos. Apparently, this ghetto had allowed parents to leave their children while they searched for food.

This area was so remote and small that when I went to the Holocaust Museum library to get information on the ghetto in Chetvertnia, I was told that there was no ghetto in Chetvertnia. But obviously I knew there had been one; Fanya Rosenblatt had told me about it. Also, before our trip, Frank had called Timothy Snyder, the Yale historian, who was an expert on Ukraine. He told Frank that the ghetto and killing in Chetvertnia was so obscure that he knew of only one person who had talked about it—Fanya. He pointed Frank to Fanya's testimonial, which I had not only read but heard the details of, from her personally, more than once.

Anna even knew the story of how my father had escaped the massacre in the ghetto, while the rest of his family had not. This, too, matched up with what Fanya had told me: that Leibel and his friend, Srulach Zilberfarb, had been sent by the Nazis to glaze windows at a train station in another town. She told me that my father was very capable and could do anything with his hands. I knew the other part of the story already: That he and Srulach had come back only to learn that everyone had been killed. That he had considered turning himself in, thinking that he'd rather be killed than live without his wife and child, but had decided, instead, to hide for a day or two. Much of the rest, of course, we don't know—and there is no one to tell us.

What Anna did say is that Davyd had remained silent and calm when the Germans came. And that at some point someone in town spotted Leibel in the house, but no one blew his cover.

Anna told us that she once saw Leibel out in the open after the war ended, when he came out of hiding. She watched him unearth a sewing machine that he'd buried in the ground, then enter his house and retrieve a basket of gold from under a floorboard beneath the kitchen table. I wondered what she was referring to, exactly, this basket of gold. Was this a Jewish stereotype, this assumption that even in a tiny village in rural Ukraine, Jews were hiding baskets of gold? Or did she simply mean he'd buried some money? Possibly even in a basket. I didn't want to probe this further. There were more important things we wanted to know from Anna.

Frank finally asked the big question: "We'd heard that Leibel and Tzipora had a baby," he said.

Anna the Old Lady replied without hesitating: "She wasn't a baby," she said. "She was a little girl, about five or six. She had long black hair and liked to play with a ball in the field."

This was stunning. Frank kept going, asking the question to which I thought I'd never have an answer. Frank asked if she knew the name of Leibel's daughter. "Of course," she said, looking straight at me. "Your sister's name was Asya."

The room was silent. I couldn't catch my breath. Now I had my sister's name, something to document her short life. A person named Asya Safran had once existed. I could imagine her outside in these fields, her long dark hair swaying as she ran for a ball.

When I returned home, I could enter her name into the Yad Vashem database, along with Tzipa and Leibel Kuperschmit. I added Asya Safran and her mother, Tzipora Safran.

Now I could also add her to the family tree.

After this revelation, there wasn't much more to say for a long while. Nadiya had prepared a vegetarian lunch for us, an enormous spread with delicious cheese dumplings, much of which she had carried with her on her long bus ride to the village. Apparently, she had spent the previous day, along with her sister-in-law and nieces, cooking and cleaning in preparation for our arrival. Anna the Old Lady, along with Anna the Translator and Ivan the Driver, joined us at the table. A bottle of vodka appeared. Ukrainian tradition has it that you fill your glass three times, for three toasts. I am a virtual nondrinker but was definitely feeling celebratory as well as grateful, and I went for all three toasts. It was quite the feast; one of Nadiya's nieces had baked a four-layer cake, teeming with cherries and candied fruits, and by the end of the meal I was not only sated but a little lit.

After lunch, gifts were produced. Mycola presented Frank with a bottle of his home-brewed vodka, and Nadiya and her sister-in-law, Svetlana, gave us hand-embroidered tablecloths.

I felt more than slightly ridiculous as I handed over our store-bought Ralph Lauren serving spoons, and it seemed not the right moment to try to explain the sentiment behind what now struck me as a lame gift. I was just grateful that I had at least brought a piece of jewelry for Nadiya. I considered giving a gift of cash, but it seemed awkward and insensitive to monetize this relationship.

After the gift exchange, we went for a walk down Krynychne Street. I tried to imagine myself strolling down this road with my father, right after the Shabbat meal, with a full belly and a slight vodka buzz and nowhere else in the world to go. Alas, there really was no place else to go—the walk was brief, because the town was small. When we reached the last house, we turned around and walked back. And then we said our farewells.

I found myself crying, and then Frank began to cry, too. Then Nadiya cried—or at least I thought she might have been crying. Frank and Mycola shared a tight embrace.

"If your family ever needs anything, just ask us. We are forever in your debt," Frank said, before we turned to leave.

Our next stop was Chetvertnia, the site of the memorial for the mass grave. Now that we had a name, I wanted to say Kaddish for my sister, Asya, and for her mother.

It was only about three miles away, but the road was especially bad, and Ivan had to concentrate hard as he drove. The village looked similar to all of the others we had seen, but when we crossed a bridge, I realized this was the place Fanya had told me about—it was where my father would have likely gone to meet the two other ghetto survivors late at night, to coordinate and strategize and commiserate after learning everyone else had been murdered.

We came to a pond with reeds and an open field and then saw steps leading to the memorial. Ivan rushed ahead to clear the site for us, but there wasn't much he could do—the place was really a mess, much more so than some of the other memorials. He and Anna were clearly ashamed by how poorly it had been kept up. The tile was corroded, and there was a broken vodka bottle on the first step, a smashed Yizkor candle on the third. It was easy to imagine the entire memorial disappearing someday, swallowed by trash and choked by weeds.

We took another New Year's card and inserted it into a crack between bricks. We were overwhelmed with conflicting emotions. This site was sacred, deeply moving, and also completely depressing.

Chetvertnia had been liquidated on October 10, 1942, I later learned from Father Desbois, who had gone with his Yahad-In Unum team in May 2012 to investigate and document the mass grave in that village. Somewhere between 100 and 120 Jews had been murdered there, not just from Chetvertnia but from the neighboring villages of Suisk, Lukow, Hodomicze, Slawatycze, and Lysche, including my sister, Asya, and her mother, Tzipora. The Germans rounded up the Jews from these villages sometime in 1941. At first, they were allowed to live in their own houses; then they were sent to a ghetto—a jammed building in Chetvertnia with a single outhouse. Jews were made to wear distinctive yellow stars on their chests and backs and were forced to work, mostly doing agricultural labor.

The Yahad team, which interviewed a witness to the murders, reported that the Jews were tied to one another, hand to hand, then led in columns to a pit that was already dug. The pit was square and near a lake. The Jews had to undress, climb down, and lie facedown on the ground. I had heard this before, of course, but now I had names to add to the terror: I could imagine my sister, Asya, with her long dark hair, holding her mother's hand.

The Germans went into the pit and shot each row of Jews, then went back to retrieve the next group. The witness reported that one Jewish man tried to escape and was killed, his body brought back by a policeman and put in the pit. Another Jew who ran away was killed on the spot and buried next to the river. Their clothes were given to villagers, and whatever was not taken was buried.

The Yahad report also says that twenty years after the shootings, the bodies of the Jews were dug up, the bones put into coffins, and reburied over a period of two days. The new burial site was supposedly where the monument was built. It reads: TO THE JEWS KILLED ON OCTOBER 10, 1942, BY GERMAN FASCISTS OF CHETVERTNIA AND SURROUNDING VILLAGES.

Our group was silent as we passed back through Krynychne. Along the way, we saw a group of women walking and realized it was Nadiya, her sister-in-law, and her nieces. They were just beginning their four-mile walk back to the bus stop—a journey that would then be followed by about two hours on the bus. We told them to hop in the van.

12

Frank and I had made our own arrangements for the next couple of days. We headed to Lviv for a bit, where we wandered the city, taking in the historic sites, observing, on the doorways, the empty holes where mezuzahs had once been. We had a chance to decompress and to absorb what we'd seen and heard. Over dinner and tea at cafés, we talked and analyzed what we had been through together. We shared an incredible experience. For Frank, that was not only a search for his grandfather's story: He told me over dinner in Lviv that the most important part of the trip for him was getting closer to me, understanding me better, and that the trip helped him fill an emotional void that he didn't even know he had.

We had moments of levity, as well, including a bit of shopping. At an outdoor market, I found a disturbing set of *matryoshka*. They were not the typical sorts of dolls, where one woman nests inside another, but rather ones that featured replicas of what were meant to be Jews. One little Jew inside another. Apparently, these were meant to be placed beside doorways in the hope that it would encourage money to flow in. It was about as anti-Semitic as one can get, but I had to have one anyway.

Bert met us at Dulles, along with Frank's wife, Abby, and his two daughters, Sadie and Theo. My mother was there, too, and she was beaming; I can still see the look on her face. Everyone was relieved to have us back, and it was good to be home. I was overwhelmed, exhausted, and emotionally drained. Part of me was back in Ukraine, some five thousand miles away, in these largely vanished villages that had loomed so large in the backdrop of my life, nearly all-consuming at times.

My mother, Sadie, Frank, Theo and I at Dulles.

It is where both of my parents' stories began, and I was eager to recount our travels and share pictures with my mother, but as with so many other conversations to do with the past, her interest was tentative. She was curious but she also wanted to forget. She would look at the pictures for a few minutes and then push them away. This scene repeated itself over and over again.

I also didn't want to burden her with too many details of

the part of the journey that had to do with my father's first family. It was his story that had always been part mystery. On this trip, finally, I had made headway in unraveling his secrets.

I confess I hadn't been to my father's grave site in years, but after that trip I paid a visit to Beth Shalom Cemetery in Capitol Heights, Maryland, where incongruous tombstones fill its hilly landscape, making the place strangely beautiful, more old Europe than suburban Maryland. My father's grave is off to the side, in the last row, in a special section reserved for deaths that are counter to the values of this Orthodox Jewish community. It made his grave easy to find as I walked along the fence at the end of the cemetery.

I needed to tell my father about the trip, that I had walked in his footsteps on the dirt roads that weave through Trochenbrod and Lysche, that I saw the pear tree in his backyard. I wanted him to know that I sat in a house now located on the same plot where his once stood, where he lived with his family, and that I came to understand, at least a little, why life was so hard for him. That I had said Kaddish for the life, and the people, he had lost. That I had mourned the things he had never spoken of to me.

I also wanted to tell him about his five beautiful grandsons and his great-grandchildren. I wanted him to know how well things turned out, despite everything that came before.

I brought rocks I had picked up in Lysche, the village where he had lived prior to the war, and some dirt from the mass graves in Chetvertnia and Trochenbrod, where I had finally learned of his secrets—or maybe they weren't secrets at all so much as a piece of his life he had found impossible to share.

To my surprise, there were already two large stones sitting atop his grave. I looked at the nearby graves, walking row by row, to see if others had stones left as reminders of a visit. None of them did. I looked at other relatives' grave sites around the cemetery and, again, nothing. Bewildered, I snapped a picture on my phone and left the reminders from my recent trip next to the large stones already there.

My father's gravestone.

I called my brother, then my mother, and my sons, to see if they had been to the cemetery. None of them had visited the grave site in years. My mother couldn't imagine who would have left stones there. This was fifty-five years after his death. There were very few people still alive who had known my father.

Jonathan proposed two options: set up a camera to see who visited the grave site next or live with the mystery. I went with the mystery.

Although I have spent a lifetime piecing together our family's fractured history, I have also learned that not every story needs a neat end, that there are times when it's okay to let the imagination fill in the gaps.

In October 2011, two years and two months after our trip, I received an email from Sergiy, Avrom's friend and one of our guides in Trochenbrod. He was eager to tell me that on a visit to Trochenbrod with other people, he had spotted the family photograph that Frank and I buried at the site of one of the memorials. Whoever found it had placed it on top of the monument, secured by two stones. Two months after his email, we heard from Anna the Translator, who also reported seeing our family photograph sprouting from the earth. This time it had been placed inside a protective plastic bag—a Ziploc, no doubt. Our photos had survived two harsh Ukraine winters and were still mostly intact. It was remarkable and yet unremarkable—the regeneration metaphor too obvious to parse.

More surprising, perhaps, is the way the connections we made on that trip continue to be part of our lives. I often wonder what my father would make of Lesia Lishcuk, the great-granddaughter of his rescuer, Davyd, sleeping in the guest room of our house. A student at the University of Kiev, she has kept in touch, and a few years after we first met at her

Uncle Mycola's house in Ukraine, she came to the United States to spend part of the summer working in Wisconsin, after which she spent a week with us.

She still signs some of her emails "from your Ukrainian family," and I reciprocate by ending mine with "from your American family." She keeps me up to date on family happenings, including new births and, sadly, the death of her Uncle Mycola.

Seventy years after Lesia's great-grandfather hid my father, I took her to meet my mother, who later had to admit, "There were some good Ukrainians."

We had dinner with Frank, his wife, Abby, and their daughters. On her last night in D.C., Lesia wanted to cook us a Ukrainian dinner. I reminded her that the meal needed to be vegetarian, which was not a problem for her—she made us borscht and potato latkes, although she called these foods by different names. It was amazing to consider that our families may have eaten the same food together around a table in Lysche.

In May 2014, after the unrest in Ukraine and the takeover of Independence Square in Kiev, Frank was part of a group that organized a conference called "Ukraine: Thinking Together"; the members included Timothy Snyder from Yale, France's Bernard-Henri Lévy, and Poland's Adam Michnik. I wrote to tell Lesia, who enthusiastically registered for the conference and spent time with Frank, including a visit to Babi Yar, where she had never been. Frank was on a panel entitled "Can memory save us from history? Can history save us from memory?" He said when he looked out at the audience and saw Lesia, he knew that he had to talk about the relationship between her family and ours and how during the darkest moments of history there were extraordinary acts of bravery. When Tim Snyder, who was moderating the panel, learned that Lesia was there, he summoned her to the stage, to loud applause.

Afterward, Lesia wrote to tell me how meaningful it was for her to be part of the conference and how touched she was by the recognition, but said, "The applause was not for me; it was for Davyd, my great-grandfather."

13

"We make Judaism tangible" is the tagline of MI POLIN, a Warsaw Judaica company founded in 2014 by Helena Czernek, a young designer, and Aleksander Prugar, a photojournalist. One of the projects they have undertaken involves scouring Poland, where more than 3.5 million Jews lived before the war, to find, on the doorposts of once-Jewish homes, traces of mezuzahs such as the ones Frank and I had seen in Lviv. A mezuzah is a decorative case with a piece of parchment inside including verses from the Torah. But each mezuzah contains more than just a bit of scripture—it embodies the story of a given house and of the family that lived there.

Touching it, they suggest, activates a link between past and present. And Czernek and Prugar do more than just channel these memories; they create, from the absence, a new presence, which is to say they actually cast in bronze a mezuzah from impressions on doorposts where the objects no longer exist.

In Trochenbrod, there are no houses left, there was no

indentation in a doorpost for a casting. The artists instead found the oldest tree, a tree that is burned on the inside but is still alive.

This spoke to me. For much of my adult life I have been haunted by the presence of absence. I gave a cast made from the tree to each of my children, and one hangs on a doorpost in my house.

There is a famous poem by the late Israeli poet Zelda Schneurson Mishkovsky: "Unto Every Person There Is a Name." We read it at the mass graves in Trochenbrod.

It's a poem that has become a song that has become a ceremony. For nearly thirty years now, on International Holocaust Remembrance Day, names of Holocaust victims are read aloud as a way of perpetuating the memory of the more than six million murdered Jews. Of restoring to them identity and dignity. "Unto every person there is a name," the poem begins. "Bestowed on him by God and given to him by his parents."

It's an impossible task, to recite all of these names, because for many of those killed, there were no survivors to remember who is gone.

For years, before our trip to Ukraine, I was obsessed with the question of how to remember my sister. Once I learned of her existence, I couldn't possibly forget her, but without a name, an age, or a physical description, I had no idea what it was I was meant to remember. I couldn't name any of my children for her or fill out a page of testimony for Holocaust victims. I couldn't create a record of any sort that spoke of her existence.

It weighed on me enough that I sought out the advice of one of the rabbis at our synagogue. How do I remember when I have nothing to remember? There was no easy answer. But one idea that emerged from our conversation was to find an object or piece of art that I could imbue with the memory of my sister, that would make me think of her when I saw it. I tucked the thought away. It seemed a good idea, but I wasn't quite sure what to do with it in practical terms.

A few months later one of my Israeli cousins, Shlomo Bisker, the son of my father's first cousin Shmuel, came for a visit with his family. They brought as a gift a lithograph by an Israeli artist; it was a picture of two girls, almost identical, wearing similar green dresses. They both have very large eyes, and they are looking out a window. One of the girls is running her fingers through a string of beads.

The artist, Yosl Bergner, is known for his allegorical work about wars, secrets, and darkness. I knew instantly this was the object that would remind me of my sister. I hung it in the dining room, across from where I usually sit, so that it would be frequently in my line of sight. For the time being, that piece of art symbolized the sister I didn't know anything about.

At the core of Judaism is the sanctification and affirmation of life. We remember, not just for the past but for the sake of the future, which speaks to the Ashkenazi tradition of naming children for those in the family who are no longer alive.

I don't remember saying my father's name out loud after he died. I probably didn't dare for fear of upsetting my mother, or maybe for fear of upsetting myself, or for fear of what I might learn.

Among the many barriers my children have helped me break down is the one about reclaiming my father's name.

Our oldest son, Franklin Louis Foer, is named for Bert's mother, Frances, who had died only months before his birth, but his middle name, Louis, is for my father. My oldest nephew is Benjamin Louis Safran. Both of our two other sons have Safran as a middle name, as does our granddaughter Theodora Safran Foer. Our first grandson, Sasha Isaiah Foer, carries my father's name in Hebrew—*Aryeh,* which means "lion." Our youngest grandson is Leo Wolf; Leo also means lion, and in Hebrew he, too, is Aryeh. The name—Leib in Yiddish, Louis in English, and Aryeh in Hebrew—lives on in two of my father's grandsons and two of his great-grandsons, which means that his name, in one form or another, is spoken in our family virtually every day.

Leo was born on October 8, 2012. He is the son of Josh and his wife, Dinah, and the first grandchild to be born after we returned from Ukraine.

This is what Josh said at Leo's bris:

Leo, my beautiful Leo Aryeh Zev. I want to tell you about my grandfather Louis, Aryeh, the man whose name you will carry with you. I want to tell you about where he came from, which is also—I pray you will never forget— part of where you come from, as well.

Grandpa Louis lived in a tiny Ukrainian shtetl called Lysche, a village of perhaps a few dozen families with just one small street. It was a town so insignificant and isolated that it could have easily been overlooked by the Nazis. But it was not.

Along with the Jews of several nearby villages,

Grandpa Louis, his wife, and their six-year-old daughter, Asya, your grandmother's half sister, were rounded up in trucks and sent to a ghetto in Chetvertnia. Grandpa Louis was known for his skill with his hands and was sometimes sent by the Nazis on work details outside of the ghetto. One day, he was returning from one of those details, fixing windows outside of town, when he received word that the ghetto had been liquidated—every last Jewish man, woman, and child had been murdered, their bodies disposed of in a mass grave. Like Job, he had lost everything: a village, a family, a daughter, a universe.

He fled into the forest and ultimately found refuge hiding in the barn of a Righteous Gentile, Davyd Zhuvniruck, whose family my mother and Frank were able to meet when they returned to Ukraine three years ago.

After the war, Louis dug up his sewing machine, and some buried gold, and started the impossible task of stitching together a new life. He made his way to Lutsk, where he met our bubbe, and then to Lodz, where my mom—your grandmother—was born. The new family escaped across the border into Germany in the false bed of a truck. My mom, a mere baby, was gagged to prevent her cries from revealing their hiding spot.

They made their way to a displaced-persons camp near Kassel, where Louis became a community leader known for his shrewd dealings in the black market.

Those who knew Louis tell of his winning personality. He was likable and got along with everybody— the kind of guy who could become friends with a table, as one survivor told my mother and brother Frank. He was, by all accounts, a loving father who doted on my Uncle Julian and my mom. But he was also frenetic. Even in America, he had never been able to stop running. He would buy a small grocery store, then sell it and buy another, only to turn around and sell it again. He couldn't rest. In 1954, just a few years after immigrating to America, he became ill and died. The war that he just barely survived had essentially destroyed him. He is enshrined today among the martyrs in the Yizkor book of Trochenbrod and Lozisht, one of the last victims of Hitler's Holocaust. He never had the opportunity to savor the freedom into which you, Leo, are being born, or to watch his children grow into great success, or to have the ultimate blessing of holding his grandchildren and great-grandchildren. But his memory will live on in you, Leo Aryeh Zev, and we pray his strength will be your strength. His warmth will be your warmth. His intelligence, your intelligence. Grandpa Louis, may your soul find rest. And may your name be a blessing for this child.

Leo, your mother and I pray that you will never forget where you come from, nor the generations who came before you. May your life be a credit to your ancestors, just as we pray that you will someday have descendants as numerous as the stars, whose lives will be a credit to you.

On the morning of Saturday, April 29, 2017, at about 3:00 A.M., Josh called to tell us that we had a new granddaughter, born minutes earlier. This, our sixth grandchild, was Leo's sister.

Mom and baby were both doing great, he assured us. He told us that they named their new daughter, Bea, after her maternal great-grandmother Debby Neumark, who had recently died. Debby's Hebrew name, Devora, translates to "bee." I was so excited that I couldn't fall back asleep, so I went downstairs.

As I entered the kitchen, I saw a yahrzeit candle that I had lit the night before. *Yahrzeit* means "time of year." While not prescribed by Jewish law, it is traditional to honor someone on the annual date of death by lighting a candle, designed to last twenty-four hours.

For a minute, I couldn't remember who the memorial candle was for. Then I was startled to realize that it was for my mother's cousin, Beatrice Shereshevsky. Even though I understood that they weren't naming our new granddaughter for this particular Bea, I was touched by the coincidence.

I managed, eventually, to fall back asleep on the sofa in our family room. A few hours later I awoke to another call from Josh. He wanted to talk more about his new daughter, and he also had a question. He asked how I would feel if Bea's middle name was Asya, after my half sister. I broke down in tears.

Months later, when my daughter-in-law Dinah was reading a draft of this book, she told me that I got one thing wrong. She and Josh had chosen the name Bea not only for her grandmother Devora but also to honor the memory of our cousin Bea and the family that made it possible for us to come to the United States.

By coincidence, or maybe not by coincidence, our new granddaughter, Bea Asya Foer, was born on the Shabbat, the Sabbath, between Yom HaShoah, the day commemorating the tragedy of the Holocaust, and Yom Ha'atzmaut, the day celebrating the birth of the state of Israel. Which is to say, between the tragedy of the past and the promise of the future. I have given her, as connective tissue, the Kiddush cup from Sura, the woman with whom my mother spent the war on the run. May her name be a blessing, and may her descendants be as numerous as the stars.

The whole family, 2018.

EPILOGUE

My mother died at almost ninety-nine years old on the eighteenth day of December, in the year 2018. In Hebrew, the numerical value of 18 translates to *chai*, which means "life." My mother, a superstitious woman, would have loved this: She was a survivor who even in her death was associated with life.

She died in our home, where she had lived for the last three and a half years, a house she had disapproved of when we bought it. It had been something of a financial reach for us at the time, and this thrifty, coupon-cutting woman thought it too extravagant. The first time I took her to see it, back in 1987, she toured the house in silence. I was eager for some form of approval—perhaps in her mind's eye she could envision her large family seated around the table in the sun-drenched kitchen or could imagine her grandchildren playing in the yard. She didn't say a word until she noticed the fence that separated the yard from the driveway. She went over and gave it a good shake, and it wobbled a bit. The fence was no good! That was all she had to say about the house.

It's an anecdote that defined our relationship—her penny-pinching and my perceived extravagance. Our inability to say what we wanted to say to each other.

It wasn't always easy those last few years, when she didn't want to live alone; with Bert's support, we brought her to live with us. We made adjustments to the house to accommodate her, including installing a motorized lift to get her up and down the stairs. I suppose part of me wanted to continue to be the good daughter, to play my role of bringing joy, to be worthy of this heroic woman. There were plenty of days, as she declined, when I asked myself how long this could go on. We had upended our lives at a time when we thought we'd be free to travel and visit grandchildren. But it was the right thing to do. I knew this in my heart, but there was also a religious and spiritual aspect to the decision: From a Jewish perspective, action is what counts. You do the right thing. The feelings come later. And they did.

It was in this house that her body lay for almost eight hours before the funeral home took her away. We wanted to surround her—her family, the rabbi, and her caregivers. We didn't leave her body alone for a second. We were waiting for Frank to return from California, where he had been on business, so that he could say goodbye. We turned on the air-conditioning, even though it was December, to keep her body cool as we watched the blood drain from her face, which began to turn a grayish white.

Somehow, we managed to comply with Jewish tradition, without quite knowing what that entailed. My brother, who is not particularly religious, somehow knew what to do, and he asked for the book of psalms to read as he sat next to her. We felt grief. We felt gratitude. We felt pride. She did it. She survived, and survived with dignity and grace. We felt her life force. Nothing felt unresolved.

Three stretch limos took the family to the funeral and the cemetery, filled with our now-large family—her children and stepchildren, their spouses, her grandchildren and their partners, and her great-grandchildren. One of the grandchildren, watching everyone pile out at the synagogue, quipped, *"Take that, Hitler!"* This is exactly what she would have said.

The synagogue was packed with hundreds of people— her friends, her children's friends, her grandchildren's friends, even the friends of her great-grandchildren, who thought of her as Bubbe, all of whom came to honor and remember. They learned new details about her, about her escape from the Nazis and her complicated life in America. She was gone, but she wasn't vanishing so much as growing bigger and more heroic as the details of her life were recalled. The word "superhero" was invoked numerous times to describe her.

Nine-year-old Cy, the youngest great-grandchild to speak at the funeral, said, "I loved everything about Bubbe. I loved the color of her hair. I loved the welcoming 'Hello, sweetie, you've grown so much since I saw you, honey.' I loved the kisses on the cheeks as if all my worries were out of me and back into the world."

My mother had made a decision a few years before her death that her final resting place would be at the old Beth Shalom Cemetery in Capitol Heights, Maryland. This is where the family that first welcomed her to America is buried. Her plot is right next to Cousin Bea, and a few steps from her Aunt Jean and Aunt Chia, and close to not-quite-four-year-old Cousin Mark, the first member of the family to be buried here. My father is buried here, as well, in a plot on the other side.

After the funeral, the rabbi invited everyone in attendance to come to the burial at the cemetery, but she warned that it would be crowded and, with its narrow, windy one-way road, somewhat difficult to access on that rainy day. It would be like a shtetl, she said. And it is a shtetl of sorts, filled with her landsmen from Kolki and Trochenbrod, many of whose names I recognize.

Her grandsons and their wives were her pallbearers. Together they carried her plain pine casket, the one mandated by Jewish tradition, meant to equalize people in death and to enable their quick return to dust. Her grandchildren carried her casket from the hearse to the grave and lovingly lowered it to the ground in the freshly dug, and very muddy, plot. We covered the casket ourselves with shovelful after shovelful of cakey, clay-like dirt. As they took turns shoveling, the boys would pause to hug one another. Each knew he had been her favorite.

The night before the funeral, I remembered the jar I had filled from the mass grave in Kolki, the one where my mother's mother, Esther, lies, along with my mother's nieces—Lifsha's daughters, Sura and Fruma Chia—and her grandparents, aunts, uncles, and cousins. I decided to bring that jar and pour its contents into her grave as a way to give her family a more dignified burial. To bring their ground to her, and her to them.

The rain picked up, and our shoes sank into the mud. I opened the jar and sprinkled dirt from nearly eight thousand miles away onto the casket. Everything was in its proper place, the earth where it belonged.

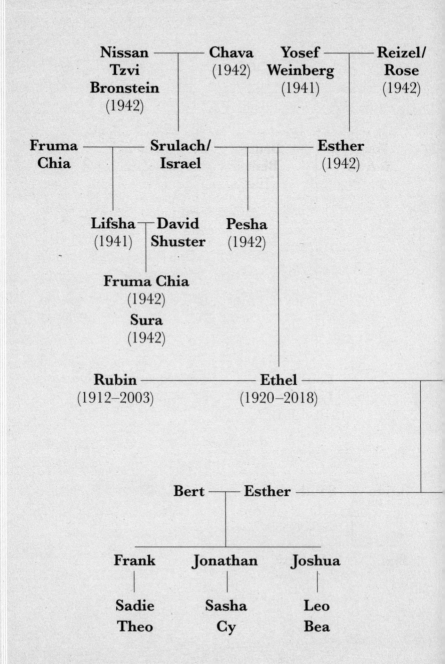

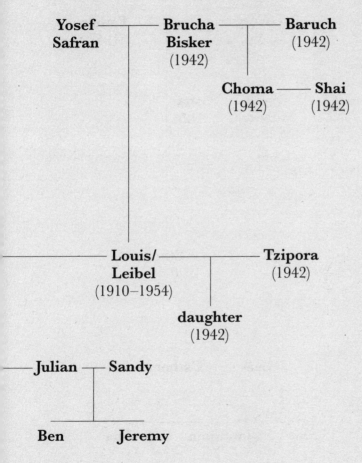

Where a single date is given, that is the date of death.

ACKNOWLEDGMENTS

Writing this book was harder than I thought and much more rewarding than I could have ever imagined. It was a journey made possible by incredible people to whom I will be forever grateful.

To my agent, Rafe Sagalyn, and my editor, Tim Duggan, who both believed in this book long before I did.

To Susan Coll, my personal editor, who became my friend. She helped lead me along the path from memory to ink.

To the terrific community of professionals at Tim Duggan Books and Crown: David Drake, Will Wolfslau, and Aubrey Martinson. Thanks to Kathy Lord, Julie Tate, Jennifer Backe, Vincent La Scala, Susan Turner, and Elena Giavaldi. And the superb publicity and marketing team of Ellen Folan, Stacey Stein, Melissa Esner, Dyana Messina, and Susan Corcoran.

To Avrom Bendavid-Val, a huge debt of gratitude for introducing me to the real story of Trochenbrod, which he recounted in his book *The Heavens Are Empty* and in the documentary *Lost Town*, created with Jeremy Goldscheider.

To the memoirists and authors who contributed to the

understanding of these places and times, among them David Schwartz, Betty Gold, David Katz, Margarete Feinstein, Robert Hilliard, and Morton Kessler.

To Sergiy Omelchuck, our guide in Trochenbrod, and to Anna Kurnyeva, our unstoppable, warm translator, researcher, and friend. Special thanks to Anna's father, Ivan, who drove us across western Ukraine.

To Natan and Itzhak Kimmelblat, in Brazil, who embraced me as a fellow Trochenbroder.

To Mira and Chaim Binnenbaum, who drove me from one end of Israel to the other to meet Trochenbroders.

To the Lischuk family in Ukraine whose grandfather, Davyd, hid my father. You are truly my Ukrainian family. Special gratitude to Lesya, who maintains contact between our families.

To Father Patrick Desbois, my hero, who has devoted his life to tracking down and documenting Holocaust mass graves in Ukraine and the former Soviet Union.

To Hannah Jopling and Gail Schwartz for their extensive interviews of my mother. And to Sarah Kaiser Hyams, who spent endless hours transcribing some of those interviews and locating documents in the Holocaust Museum's database.

To the readers who helped improve the book at every phase, including Jackie Leventhal, David Marwell, Louise Myers, Anat Bar-Cohen, Barbara Heller, Marge Mueller, Amy Oringel, and my newly found cousin Cheryl Kahn.

To my husband, Bert, who supports and encourages me in everything I do. Nothing would be possible without Bert—my life, our family, and this book, which he read many times as the drafts mounted. Bert made it possible for me to take care of my mother in the last years of her life. I know that she loved him. In a family of secrets, she would pull him aside and say, "Esther and Julian don't tell me anything. I need for you to tell me what is going on."

To our three sons, each of whom played a key role in the evolution of this story.

• Jonathan, who unlocked the door with *Everything Is Illuminated*.

• Frank, who was the first member of our family to write my mother's story. Frank also took the trip with me to Ukraine and continues to travel the journey.

• Josh, who got the last word with the naming of Leo and Bea Asya.

To my grandchildren, who inspire me every day to keep memory alive.

ABOUT THE AUTHOR

ESTHER SAFRAN FOER was the CEO of Sixth & I, a center for arts, ideas, and religion. She lives in Washington, D.C., with her husband, Bert. They are the parents of Franklin, Jonathan, and Joshua, and the grandparents of six.